THE OTHER CHINA

THE OTHER CHINA
Journeys around Taiwan

৪৩

Douglas Fetherling

ARSENAL PULP PRESS
VANCOUVER

THE OTHER CHINA
Copyright © 1995 by Douglas Fetherling

ARSENAL PULP PRESS
103-1014 Homer Street
Vancouver, B.C.
Canada V6B 2W9

The publisher gratefully acknowledges the assistance of the Canada Council and the Cultural Services Branch, B.C. Ministry of Small Business, Tourism and Culture.

Cover design by Gek-Bee Siow
Printed and bound in Canada

CANADIAN CATALOGUING IN PUBLICATION DATA:
Fetherling, Douglas, 1949-
The other China

ISBN 1-55152-025-7

1. Fetherling, Douglas, 1949- —Journeys—Taiwan. 2. Taiwan—Description and travel. I. Title.
DS799.24.F47 1995M   915.124'9045   C95-910825-4

Contents

My thanks to the editors who encouraged me on these

voyages of inquiry by being kind enough to publish some

of my rough notes: Carol Martin of The Canadian

Forum, Laszlo Buhasz of The Globe and Mail, and

Neil Reynolds of the late Whig-Standard Magazine.

Prologue

I am standing on the spot where the Third World War almost broke out—twice. I am on the island of Kinmen, which was then known as Quemoy. Kinmen is one of two tiny subsidiary islands (the other, Matsu, retains its old name) that were the subject of an ongoing dispute between the Chinese nationalists of the Republic of China on Formosa (now Taiwan) and the Chinese communists of the People's Republic of China. I am on my second sojourn in Taiwan, completing a self-assigned mission to make a complete circuit of the island. The visit to Kinmen is a side-trip but, to me, a vitally important one.

Kinmen, about 1,200 kilometres from the Taiwanese capital of Taipei, is only three kilometres wide at its narrowest and approximately twenty kilometres long; it is a low, desolate sort of place, a brown-and-green land of sand dunes and caves, of razor wire and camouflaged bunkers, and it is surrounded on three sides by fingers of the communist mainland. At high tide, the two ideologies are separated by only 2.2 kilometres of water; at low tide, 1.7. I have clambered up onto one of

Kinmen's uncountable defensive works to squint across the water at members of the People's Liberation Army who, I have no doubt, are squinting back at me. Such situations impart an eerie feeling.

In a sense, my generation has grown up with the events that happened, or threatened to happen, here. In 1949, the Chinese civil war finally ended when Generalissimo Chiang Kaishek abandoned Mainland China to his old adversary Mao Zedong and retreated. Chiang took the entire infrastructure of his Kuomintang (or Nationalist Party) with him, and reassembled it on the offshore province of Formosa, only recently returned to China after a half-century occupation by the Japanese. Assured of continued U.S. support simply because he opposed communism, Chiang dug in and awaited developments (while misappropriating billions of U.S. dollars—1940s and 1950s U.S. dollars—for the benefit of the Chiang family).

Chiang didn't have to wait long. In October 1949, Quemoy was attacked by 10,000 communist troops, who were repelled by the Nationalists. There was always the fear, the danger, the presumption, that the U.S. would come to the Nationalists' aid militarily, not just economically, as it would continue to do for another thirty years.

The touchiest moment was August 23, 1958, when Mao's troops tried again. On the ground, the two sides engaged in an artillery duel that lasted forty-four days; in the skies, the Nationalist air force, showing what was called the *chien-chia* spirit of the Second World War, shot down thirty-two Soviet-made MiG-17s. One day, three Nationalist generals were killed by an exploding shell; Chiang's life was spared only because he had gone back for his hat.

The crisis atmosphere waxed and waned but never seemed to vanish. Today, the 1960 presidential debates between John F. Kennedy and Richard Nixon are remembered as a test of the candidates' telegenic attributes. We've forgotten that one of their major arguments was over the crisis on Quemoy and Matsu. As recently as the late '70s, the two Chinas were still firing artillery shells at each other (although only on alternating days, so as to conserve ammunition).

The Taiwanese still have 30,000 very lonely troops on tiny Kinmen (and another 100,000 in reserve, ready to be moved there on short notice). But the tension between the rivals, each claiming to be the legitimate heir to Sun Yat-sen's overthrow of the last imperial dynasty in 1912, has changed focus. It has changed focus geographically (recently, the potential flash-point in the war of words between the two contenders has moved to the Spratly Islands in the South China Sea). But it has changed focus politically as well. There is current talk in Taiwan of turning Kinmen into a tourist area (an idea I can't imagine working unless the planners visualize a Cold War theme park).

Some thought Prime Minister Pierre Trudeau's official recognition of the People's Republic of China in 1970 was the beginning of the end for Taiwan's claim to importance, especially when President Richard Nixon, for his own reasons, followed suit in 1979, recognizing the government at Beijing and cutting off the one at Taipei. There the stand-off remained until two other trends began to emerge.

One was the sound of a ticking clock growing louder. Everyone knew that in 1898 the British had taken a lease on most of Hongkong for only ninety-nine years. As 1997 drew nigh, the whole complexion of Asian politics began to change. Beijing's massacre of thousands of pro-democracy demonstrators at Tiananmen Square in 1989 only increased fears of what sort of repressive measures might be brought to bear on a Hongkong grown used to British-style democracy.

In Beijing, Deng Xioping had been experimenting with vast economic reforms (such as ending communal farming, and encouraging limited capitalism, including stock markets). But these changes brought no significant improvement in human rights. To be sure, life was better in Mainland China than during the terror of the Cultural Revolution in the 1960s, but no better than it had to be to keep the peace. Beijing had promised that Hongkong would have special status within the People's Republic, for it was, and is, a valuable magnet for hard currency. (Controlling Hongkong is like owning a giant casino.) But to people living in the colony, the prospect of being run by the People's Liberation Army was not a happy one. The result was a great new Chinese diaspora which changed the faces of such cities as Vancouver and Sydney, making them wealthier than they had ever been.

Another of the urban centres to benefit, although somewhat differently, was Taipei, which hoped (and hopes) to gain if Hongkong turns sour under the communists, by becoming a safe harbour for free enterprise and state-of-the-art communications. Even if Hongkong is grafted back onto the body of China successfully, the Taiwanese, or some of them, still stand to benefit. If Hongkong can be smoothly re-integrated into the life of Mainland China after only one hundred years, then why not Taiwan after only fifty?

These questions describe the schematic lines around Taiwanese politics. One faction of the ruling Kuomintang (much improved from the KMT of Chiang Kai-shek but still in power despite the end of martial law and the beginning of democracy in the late 1980s) continues to maintain, officially at least, that Taipei is the capital of all China. Younger people, most of them born after their parents' or grandparents' relocation to the island, reject even the faintest trace of this polite fiction. They seek to declare a new and second Chinese republic that would scheme and beg for admittance to the United Nations, the World Bank, and other international bodies.

Any move in such a direction, however, provokes a near-violent response from the People's Republic. The most recent manifestation started in the spring of 1995 and has sunk Sino-American relations to their lowest level since the Tiananmen shootings. For sixteen years, Taiwanese officials had been refused entry to the U.S. for fear of irritating the People's Republic. But with the Republicans resurgent in Congress, a decision was made to allow Taiwanese President Lee Teng-hui to appear in Ithaca, New York, as a private citizen, to make a non-partisan convocation address at Cornell University, his alma mater. Beijing was furious. In the West, the slick and patient Taiwan lobby was delirious. Both sides saw Lee's visit as the thin edge of the wedge. Which is why standing on Kinmen is charged with such symbolism.

Metaphorically, the gap of 1.7 kilometres is either about to widen considerably, or to close up entirely.

Early in 1996, probably in March, Taiwan will be holding its first-ever free election for national president. This is an election that Canadians should pay attention to for several reasons. It will affect the face of what is virtually the only country in east Asia where human rights and democracy, while far from perfect, are rapidly improving. More parochially, the vote could affect one of the trading partners with whom Canada's relationship is growing. By 2020, total economic activity in east Asia will exceed the combined total for Europe and North America. Taiwan is one of our best opportunities to wring some advantage from a transition we can do little to influence.

But I was also drawn to write about Taiwan for its own sake. This nation or province (the term you choose reveals your sympathies) has had a turbulent and schizophrenic past but is now at some sort of crossroads, for the ambitious capitalist state that has become one of the Asia's great economic powerhouses is also a self-conscious semi-nation struggling for respect in the shadow of its nearest neighbour. Something about Taiwan will strike Canadians as familiar.

1991

My timing is impeccable, as usual. People keep apologizing, saying, "This is the last typhoon of the season," as though I have arrived just a few days earlier than I should have to discover their dirty little secret. The long flight from Los Angeles took no cognizance of Typhoon Ruth, as this one has been named by its proud parents at the Central Weather Bureau. By the time we arrive at Taipei, however, the storm is moving northwest from the top of the Philippines, across the Bashi Channel. Such is the usual avenue.

There was probably never any fear that Ruth would trigger one of the official CWB Emergency Alerts ("Move furniture away from windows . . . roll up rugs and place them on the furniture"). But a Condition 24 is certainly likely ("Fill your vehicle with gasoline"), perhaps a Condition 12 ("Store extra drinking water"), maybe even an old-fashioned Condition 6 ("Do not travel unless necessary"). Like the evil spirits of Chinese mythology that move straight lines, the storm loses much of its power by making a sharp change in direction, until it is travelling at sixty metres a second over a 300-kilometre front. Its main effects seems to be this extraordinary rain, which gives every pedestrian a perfectly horizontal shower bath, and the fact that 700 tourists are stuck on the Pescadores, in the Taiwan Strait, and on Lanyü and the other islands on the Pacific side. Alas, those are my destinations.

The little twenty-eight-seat aircraft that make the one-hour trip to those places are grounded. When the storm passes, they stay in their hangars one more day, for prudence's sake. Then yet another day, just in case, while I twiddle my thumbs in the capital, window-shopping, reading the newspapers, staying out of trouble. Then no amount of coaching can bring the planes out, at least for as long as I remain in Taiwan. "You would require a guide and the guides don't go at this time of year," the Government Information Office tells me. I have come just at the moment when summer becomes winter. So I sit down to enjoy some winter days in Taipei, where at least the politics are interesting. It's always a good time to observe politics in Taipei, where in recent years fistfights and brawls have become common in the legislature.

€)Ч

In 1949, the communists drove Chiang Kai-shek and his Kuomintang political apparatus, his army and supporters, from mainland China to the offshore province of Formosa, about 160 kilometres away. From then until 1989, the two countries were officially at war. On occasion, there would be threats of violence to back up the mere theory. The tension level was not directly related to the fevers and bouts of hypothermia which made up the cold war in Europe. But the cycle was similar, because at base the antagonists were the same. On the one hand, there were the Americans who had been pouring money into Chiang's army and government since the 1920s in an effort to maintain China as a right-wing totalitarian country, and on the other, America's supposed nemesis, the worldwide communist conspiracy (Chinese branch). In more recent times, as other concerns came to occupy Washington's attention, in Asia and elsewhere, the standoff in China cooled, but in cooling it solidified ever harder, like lava turning into obsidian. Even after Chiang's death in exile in 1975 (an exile he made into a kind of rival reality), the Taiwanese Nationalists and the Mainland communists would still cling to their respective policy-fictions.

The People's Republic of China claims to consist of twenty-two provinces—twenty-one on the Mainland and the rebellious Taiwan a short distance across the water. Taiwan, for its part, has claimed with equal conviction for the past forty-two years to be the real China, the Republic of China, from which the other twenty-one provinces have broken away, with their illegitimate and bogus government in Beijing (which Taiwan calls Peking, refusing to adopt the Mainland's romanization reforms). In the official view of Taiwan and the Kuomintang (or, in the Mainland spelling, Guomintang) which still rules it, this island is not the home of a government-in-exile but of the legitimate Republic of China established by Sun Yat-sen in 1912 following the overthrow of the last imperial dynasty, the Ching. The fact that Taiwan is less than 400 kilometres long and has twenty percent fewer people than Canada, while the People's Republic is 9.6 million square kilometres and has 1.2 billion people, a quarter of the world's population, does not influence the mutual make-believe, the suspension of belief that was American policy from the start and continued until Richard Nixon recognized the People's Republic, and Taiwan's diplomatic integrity started to bleed away.

America has long maintained its own double standard with a two-China policy (first postulated by Canada in 1966). This was useful during the Vietnam War when Taiwan was needed as an ally in a hostile region (and as yet another R and R site). In 1978, with the Vietnam War over, Jimmy Carter called a halt to America's part in the charade by ending U.S. diplomatic relations with Taiwan in order to placate the People's Republic. Taiwan then withdrew from the United Nations, refusing to take part as long as the People's Republic was a member. Today, Taiwan enjoys normal official relations with few other countries but vigorous trade with many, making do with a tangle of trade missions, foreign chambers of commerce, and other subdiplomatic structures to facilitate communication and consular necessity.

So the Asian cold war has lingered on. It is coming to a conclusion only now, owing not to the economic collapse of one side (as in Europe) but rather thanks to an economic boom on the other. Taiwan has a per capita income of about US$20,000 (as against about $24,000 in the United States itself), and is now the world's twelfth largest economy (Canada ranks seventh). Of all the Asian economies, including Singapore, South Korea, and Thailand, only Japan has had faster growth. Taiwanese are still forbidden to trade with the Mainland directly, but through intermediaries in Hongkong they now own 3,000 factories and other businesses in the People's Republic. Like Americans relocating below the Mexican border, they are going where labour is cheap and environmental laws are lax. And there is the added dimension of racial, national, and familial loyalty as well.

A number of Asian countries are referred to in the media as "economic miracles." In Taiwan's case, the miracle has certain appealing aspects not so easily associated with other places where there's a Rolex on every wrist and a Rolodex on every desk. When Chiang set about digging in at his fortress of an island, Taipei was a poky, dusty place of low stucco buildings with red tile roofs. (You can see a few of them yet, hiding in the shadows of the office blocks and hotels that line its straight wide boulevards.) Its population was only 600,000 and people got around by bicycle or three-wheeled pedicab. Today, with slightly fewer people than Toronto, Taipei has more taxis than either London or Paris, and is materialistic to a fault but not to the point of pathology like Hongkong or Tokyo. The crowds and the traffic are a nightmare to be made worse for the next ten years by construction of an enormous elevated rapid transit system. But it's peaceful and clean next to Bangkok, say. And while the Kuomintang continue to reign, Taiwan as compared to Singapore is no longer a particularly authoritarian place, or at least it's become far less so recently. The instructional video shown on incoming China Air flights is out of date in suggesting that strict foreign exchange controls are still observed or that one can't bring in *Playboy* or decks of playing cards. Taiwan is wallowing in foreign exchange reserves, and at one point the government even tried operating casinos to encourage tourism in remote areas: an experiment that failed only because it wasn't making enough profit. Only murder and kidnapping still carry the death penalty, making Taiwan far more liberal in this respect than the United States.

Under Chiang Kai-shek and his family, there were opposition parties in Taiwan in name only. But now there is a real one, the Democratic Progressive Party. There is also freedom of expression. Although eighty percent of the press is still controlled by the KMT, the remaining twenty percent is unmuzzled to a remarkable extent—certainly as compared with television, which is still licensed by the Ministry of Defense. There are movements towards a new kind of democracy—halting, uncertain, sometimes grudging steps, but the thrust is clear. In this instance they seem inseparable from the rise in living standards, education, and general prosperity. In one long generation, the Fujianese and Guangdongese who fled to Taiwan have done amazingly well for themselves. Now in their twilight years, some of them are beginning to look back at the land of their youth, where many already have investments. This pragmatic nostalgia is becoming a powerful force in the politics of Taiwan and the region, but the island and the Mainland have had a longer, more intricate relationship than most of us with comparatively little pasts have realized.

Typhoon Ruth never rises to its full potential (nor does Seth, which follows immediately), but neither does it go away. The manager of the nondescript hotel where I am staying sets up a visual aid in the lobby, a plywood map on which he can plot the storm's progress by moving a red ball higher up the display, like a local United Way chairperson showing how much money has been collected thus far and what the goal is. My hosts are probably right to be concerned. Conditions to the south remain unpredictable. On the third day, a freighter bound from Hongkong to Taichung is thought to have gone down in heavy seas near the Penghu archipelago, or the former Pescadores, with eighteen crew members missing (in fact, it has run aground and all are rescued). For the time being we will remain in the north and I will look elsewhere for what I am seeking, which is some place that shows in sedimentary strata some of the pre-Kuomintang history of Taiwan. A pretty consistent history it is, too. Hundreds of years before the communist revolution, the island seems always to have been someone's refuge and the refuge in turn a provocation to the conquerors from whom they had fled.

Most Taiwanese live on the coastal plain facing the Mainland, which is industrial and agricultural by turns. The plain on the Pacific side is much narrower and less productive (cement and marble quarrying are its two big industries). It is therefore less populous as well. The middle of the island is taken up by the Central Mountain Range, which keeps cross-island communications rather basic, especially during landslide season. In the half-light of a misty morning, these mountains, rising two, three, even four thousand metres in one case, look like they've come to life from a scroll painting.

In the mountains and in some of the places around the edges, and on islands such as Lanyü, live a large but diverse group of aboriginal peoples, descendants of those who came originally from the Philippines and other spots to the south or from Polynesian islands far to the east. These peoples were driven into the mountains by the Hakka, a despised minority from northern China who had been pushed off the Mainland and across the Strait. The descendants of the Hakka still constitute about five percent of Taiwan's population. Taiwan has been a nest used by successive generations of birds, each forced out by the next—until now. It was the same with the Europeans when they arrived.

The Portuguese got there first (hence place names such as Formosa and the Pescadores), but they had the island to themselves as a staging area for the China trade for only a few years, until 1624, when the Dutch East India Company established itself on the southwest coast. In 1641 the Dutch forcibly put an end to a Spanish incursion in the north and became thereby masters of all the commercially desirable ports of the island for the next twenty years.

Taiwan has three national heroes of ultra-legendary status. In reverse chronological order, they are Chiang Kai-shek, his mentor Dr Sun Yat-sen, the founder and first president of the Chinese republic, and Cheng Chenhkung, a Ming general and sometime pirate who defeated the Dutch in 1661. Like Chiang 200 years later, Cheng, who is usually called Koxinga in English (on the Mainland, Coxinga), was blown across the Strait by events he could no longer control. The arrival of the Manchus from the north having put an end to the Ming dynasty, Koxinga fled to Taiwan with 30,000 soldiers in 800 war junks. Six months later he had driven the Dutch from the island and began dreaming, like Chiang Kai-shek after him, of reconquering the Mainland. But instead, the Mainland invaded Taiwan (as had been about to happen to Chiang when the Korean War intervened and the Americans interposed the Seventh Fleet between the two enemies). Now the Mainland itself was a kind of colonizing force and Taiwan, as usual, the unwilling host. Not until 1887, when it already had a population of 2.5 million, did Taiwan become a full province of imperial China, rather than a mere county of Fujian province.

෴

With Typhoon Ruth now downgraded to mere tropical-storm status, but with the wind still kicking up, I set off northward out of Taipei along the Tanshui River to the town of the same name, a not very popular tourist destination where much of Taiwan's history converges in a cluster of buildings called Fort San Domingo. I've always been attracted to structures that bear the cumulative traces of sequential occupation, particularly if the remnants are highly improbable or contradictory. There's a building on a side-street in downtown Toronto, once a synagogue, which I've watched become a Korean Baptist church, a community crisis bureau, and a day-care centre, as the texture of the neighbourhood has changed. Not far away is the site of a tiny storefront, now razed, which I can remember being the headquarters of every conceivable political group over the years, not excluding the Trotskyites. Fort San Domingo is similar in a way.

As its name suggests, this mountain outpost overlooking the sea to Kuanyin Mountain is evidence of the brief Spanish interlude in Taiwan, practically the only such evidence left today. The Spanish rebuilt it following an attack by the aboriginals. It fell to the Dutch soon enough (which explains its Chinese name still in use today: *Hung Mao Ch'eng*, "the castle of the red-haired people"). Then the Chinese under Koxinga took over. Each time it was destroyed the town was rebuilt in a different style. This is what gives Fort San Domingo its charm—this and the fact that it occupies such a peaceful spot. A Spanish arch standing on a Dutch foundation that postdates it is one of the anomalies that resulted. Actually it's an exaggeration to call it a fort at all, much less a castle. It's a kind of stout two-storey blockhouse. But in truth, it's hard to tell what it must have looked like at any of its previous turning points because it was remade yet again in the nineteenth century, this time by the British, who leased it in perpetuity in 1867. A tablet that was once part of the complex but now stands apart, like an old tombstone detached from its proper place, bears the inscription *V.R. 1868*.

This was in the age of the Treaty Ports following China's humiliation in the Opium Wars and the Taiping Rebellion when the European colonial powers, and the Japanese, too, won extraordinary concessions from the Ching rulers. Tanshui, though it was then the largest port on Taiwan, still remained pretty much off the beaten path of British hegemony. But the Americans, by this time the great rivals of the British in the China trade, had been sniffing about and indeed would probably have simply snatched Taiwan outright if it hadn't been for their Civil War at home. So both the British and the Americans kept consular missions in Tanshui. In 1891, the British went so far as to add a quite splendid official residence on the grounds, a two-storey affair with Romanesque touches, similar to some in the old fort, part of which was now a gaol for British subjects (who, under the principle of extraterritoriality, were immune from Chinese law).

Although it does not lie in the same county as the capital, Tanshui has long since lost its identity as a distinct city. It still relies heavily on its fishing fleet for sustenance, and a long row of seafood restaurants lines the highway. The community is also a bedroom development for Taipei, and the one road that links the two places no longer offers much countryside to look at, just urban sprawl. Given the waning of British power in the Pacific, and Tanshui's decline into civic irrelevance, it is surprising that the Foreign Office in Whitehall kept the consulate open until 1972, after which they gave it over to the Australians, who passed it on to the Americans, before, finally, in 1984, it became a museum.

It is an anomaly whichever way you look at it. Fort San Domingo, with its hints of ancient diplomatic intrigue (two wall-safes, one very old indeed, and a primitive stove for incinerating documents), is a babble of different periods and architectural styles, a kind of folly almost, such as an eccentric lord might have built from scratch, imitating the caprice of history to make a centrepiece for the gardens of his vast estate.

And then there is the consular residence, with its reception-
and morning-rooms and separate quarters for staff and servants. By the look of it, the British must have left much of the
furniture when they finally decamped.

Curiously, Taiwan, with its violent past, is as poor in old
fortifications as peaceful Bermuda, say, is rich. San Domingo
is very far from the most complete, and is not really what it
claims to be at all. Its importance is simply that it occupies a
spot—a lovely spot, high above Shalun Beach, where surfers
cavort during certain seasons—where so many of the currents
of early Taiwanese history happen to come together: the
Spanish and the Dutch traders, the aboriginals, the first defi-
nite influx of Chinese under Koxinga, but not, curiously, the
British themselves. In stark distinction to the Chinese Mainland and the forces that shaped it, Taiwan is a place in whose
development the British played almost no role (and the
French even less). The Americans were always the rulers and
the cultural models here—the Americans and the still-hated
Japanese, who took the island in 1895 and ran it ambitiously
but with a certain cruelty until forced to cede it back to China
at the end of the Second World War.

This is another reason that the old consulate is so interesting: one is hard-pressed to find the slightest sign of British
civilization in Taiwan, while signs of the American equivalent
are so abundant that they seem almost natural. The floor above
the ground floor is called the second, not the first. Yet there

is no triskaidekaphobia as in North America: the tall buildings all have thirteenth floors. Many of them, however, do lack fourth floors, and houses with four storeys are difficult to sell, owing to bad *feng shui*. Advertisements calling for applicants with American accents reflect more than simply the ubiquity of CNN. How unusual it is for Americans to find themselves not the most disliked of foreigners in a place. Yet that's not to say they're perforce the most admired, at least not distinctly so.

There was a time, 250 years ago, when Formosa was all the rage among the British intellegentsia, in whose midst had appeared a charismatic foreigner named George Psalmanazar, a friend of Samuel Johnson's. Psalmanazar, who claimed to be a citizen of Formosa, had written a very popular (and completely counterfeit) history of the place and was soon teaching a language which he called Formosan to Oxford divinity students training as missionaries. In 1747 he confessed publicly to having made it all up, and he became known, in the words of his biographer, as "one of the most succesful liars of all time."

Today, English is taught in Taiwanese schools from the earliest levels as a matter of pragmatism, though with wildly varying success, of course, and a degree from an American or at least a Canadian university is almost *de rigueur* in certain professions and for those aspiring to public life in the generation that lies ahead. Some of the preferred schools might sound odd; the University of Missouri, for example, is an enclave of ambitious Taiwanese. Citizens now sixty or older are likely to speak Japanese as well, as a result of the long occupation. Recently when a young reporter from *Asahi Shimbun* or *Yomiuri Shimbun* or some other Japanese newspaper came to interview Premier Hua Pei-tsun in his office in the Presidential Building (built by the Japanese before the war, like the Foreign Ministry and other public structures in Taipei), he found that they could communicate quite effectively without the presence of a translator. This eliminated the premier's young Taiwan-born aides, who sat in on the meeting but had no idea what was taking place.

This strikes me as a telling anecdote. While being thoroughly Chinese, the people of Taiwan are struggling to make something quite new from the mixture of qualities they admire in America and Japan, both economically and now, more slowly, politically as well. So far the resulting social concoction is much more pleasant than either of the ingredients on their own might lead one to expect, though it has not been without its problems, not by any means.

ಐಂ

The rain is still coming down like a waterfall and the wind looks ready to start tearing the leaves off the palmettos. I tell my Taiwanese companion, a young communications student who has agreed to serve as translator and explainer, that I have never been in a typhoon before, not even in what they call a baby typhoon. A hurricane alert in Florida once is the nearest sensation I have experienced. He tells me about the most recent typhoon and also entertains me with his favourite earthquake memories.

"Do they have such things in your country?" he asks.

"Our disasters are usually man-made," I reply.

"Ah, politics," he says. "We have those here as well."

Before the end of the year there will be an election in Taiwan; the oddsmakers, seeing the Kuomintang's almost uncanny ability to embrace just enough change to stay in power, are predicting a victory for the admittedly somewhat volatile status quo. The issues are democracy, nationalism, and the generation gap. The last of these, in a curious way, actually provides the key to the other two.

In 1948, President Chiang Kai-shek announced a "period of communist rebellion." This was a state-of-siege declaration, giving extraordinary powers to him and the Kuomintang. The next year, he and the government, faced with defeat by the communists, retreated to Taiwan and settled in for a long rule. Chiang was genuine in his hatred of the communists. To the Americans, this was more important than his affection for fascism or something very close to it, and he used this fact to squeeze all the money from them that he could. As Harry Truman is supposed to have said, "He may be a son-of-a-bitch, but he's our son-of-a-bitch." In fairness, Chiang could have expressed precisely the same sentiment about Truman—or Eisenhower or Kennedy or Johnson or Nixon . . . but there the chain stopped. Nixon recognized the People's Republic as the real China, and in 1978, a few years after Chiang died and was succeeded by family and friends, Taipei broke diplomatic relations with Washington. Only since 1987, when the Emergency Decree, as martial law was called, was lifted, has life been growing freer, particularly under Lee Teng-hui, the current president. The situation is hardly without its tensions, however, as the government tries to maintain change at the present pace and its antagonists try to speed it up.

Mr Lee was mayor of Taipei and governor of Taiwan Province before achieving the presidency. But the most significant line on his CV is the fact that, although he's sixty-eight years old, he is—in the sense of having been born in Taiwan and not on the Mainland—a member of the younger generation. For it is on this point of birthplace that the generation gap comes into play and informs, even defines, the future of the constitution.

As part of the hypothesis that Taiwan is the real China and the People's Republic an imposter, the National Assembly in Taipei has always been run by persons born on the Mainland. Nominally, they represent not just Taiwan but the other twenty-one provinces as well. Such Mainland-born people, together with their Taiwanese-born offspring, make up only about fifteen percent of the population. Until now, they have held eighty percent of the seats in the Assembly—held them indefinitely, while controlling the mechanisms for amending the constitution. The same situation also prevailed in the other, less powerful chamber, the Legislative Yuan. There had always been a few small political parties (such as the Labour Party, whose most famous member gathers a crowd on the hustings by performing a striptease act). But the first real one wasn't founded until 1986, and didn't begin to gain great strength (thirty percent of the popular vote in the last election) until after suspension of martial law.

The Democratic Progressive Party is unusually named in that it is actually democratic and progressive. It favours direct election of a simplified government instead of the current system in which the president appoints the premier, who then appoints the ministers. The Democratic Progressives are also dominated by native-born Taiwanese who are usually far younger than Mr Lee and without his commitment to business as usual. The most controversial plank in the DPP platform calls for an end to the hopes of reuniting the two Chinas with Taiwan having the most power. It proposes simply declaring Taiwan an independent republic, seeking readmittance to the United Nations and otherwise getting on with the realities of life.

It's dangerous to generalize too much about either party. The Kuomintang, for example, includes everyone from relative liberals to former brownshirts—as does the DPP itself, by way of being a coalition of sorts. But on the fundamental question of "independence" not from some old colonial power but from old romantic ideology, there is a clear polarity that need not be tinctured by too much qualification. All other questions—the necessity of direct representation and what kind of constitution is best—flow from that. The DPP adopted its position on the matter at some danger to its members, given that Mr Lee still controls the formidable anti-subversion machinery and hasn't hesitated to use it in the past.

The DPP is certainly driven in part by a grass-roots pro-democracy sentiment similar to that which the communists crushed on the Mainland. But the way the KMT has met the threat more closely resembles the situation in Poland or the former U.S.S.R. in recent memory: they have permitted dissent, but only up to a point. And necessity keeps changing what that point is. For example, one of the important opposition leaders, Hsu Sin-liang, was a political prisoner not all that long ago. Yet much of the agitation has to be done from bases overseas. People from those bases who return to Taiwan do so at their peril, as when Kuo Pei-hung, leader of the U.S. branch of the exiled group called World United Formosans for Independence, slipped in recently and was promptly arrested. The case that made the biggest splash in Canada was that of Y.S. Leo, a Toronto bank analyst who returned to Taipei and was charged with false entry. Later, after Joe Clark refused to listen to a plea on Yeo's behalf from the United Nations, a charge of sedition was added. Mr Leo is the only Canadian citizen ever designated a "prisoner of conscience" by Amnesty International.

The DPP's historic decision to make an independence plebiscite part of its policy was taken at a party convention on October 13. The next day, the government began ferreting out still more oppositionists, as the local press calls them. By the time I arrive almost three weeks later, the total of newly arrested leaders stands at eleven and is climbing. Meanwhile, the cabinet rules the DPP plan for a vote on independence illegal and orders it be changed or else. The "or else" is taken by some in the DPP to mean that their party will be disbanded. This tough talk is clearly designed in part to placate Beijing.

Until the massacre at Tiananmen Square and the world's reaction to it, the standard interpretation of Chinese-Taiwanese relations was this: that hard-line communists on the Mainland relish the thought of reunification on their own terms as much as KMT hard-liners cherish the quixotic dream of reunification on theirs. Of course, acting on either is a very different matter. But as the pro-independence movement has grown more vociferous, so has the People's Republic made a display of becoming restive. At length, Beijing went so far as to make at least a thinly veiled threat to invade Taiwan if the island ever does declare independence. To sensitive individuals, the whole notion sounds quite far-fetched. The same folks who could get back Hongkong merely by waiting for a century, or get back Macao by waiting for five centuries, aren't likely to fly off the handle—especially given that they are still smarting from the world's criticism of the one instance when they did indeed overact so terribly in putting down their own student protesters. The KMT, however, has used this ominous statement to justify its crackdown on the DPP policy, while extending the deadline for its repeal.

Yet even as these deadlines are being ignored, the Mainland has taken the unusual step of commissioning a public poll on the subject of Taiwan—and the still more unusual step of releasing the results. The survey shows that fifty-eight percent of those asked feel that the People's Republic should not interfere in the course of Taiwan's political future. Finally, but well before the last deadline, the DPP rejects the demand that it rescind its policy. And nothing happens, except that more people are arrested and some of those arrested are deported back to exile.

The Asian equivalent of perestroika will continue on its own timetable, slowly but steadily, without any of the unexpected and violent turns seen elsewhere, both sending a signal to, and taking a signal from, the concurrent example of the two Koreas, which sometimes seem to be moving towards their own kind of reconciliation. That's where the matter rests at this writing, when local turf accountants are giving odds that despite the probability of large DPP gains in the December election, matters will still unfold slowly, with the country, having already moved away from sham elections, progressing towards elections in the Chicago manner and from there maybe to real democracy, when the generation of 1948-49 has been voted out by the surest force in politics, a wave of what might be called actuarial reform. That won't be all that much longer, when you think of it. After all, Chiang Kai-shek's *grandson* (who lives in Canada) is well past retirement age.

Having put in motion its own eventual obsolescence, the KMT has also set loose an elaborate plan to postpone the day of reckoning as long as possible. Just weeks after declaring an end to the forty-year "war" with the Mainland (and delicately sidestepping the issue of who won), President Lee and his more conservative premier, Hau Pei-tsun, announced implementation of the Six-Year Plan. This is a public works scheme of unprecedented size and scope, designed to plough a lot of Taiwan's new commercial wealth back into the country—and make the KMT all the more difficult to remove from power. New highways, railway systems, and airports are being built, along with new shopping centres and parks, to a total of about US$300 billion. The opposition will be hard-pressed to whip up dissatisfaction with go-getting on such a grand scale as this.

But the KMT knows that it must do something else as well: address the insecurity of so many Taiwanese, young ones especially, who have grown up in an atmosphere of isolation from the West and a sense of betrayal by the U.S. and others. They are the people who provide grass-roots support for the DPP's vision of a new kind of nationalism, totally different from that of Chiang in his day, based on pride in material achievement against what were for so long such overwhelming odds. The change began in the late 1980s when Taiwanese were permitted to travel freely to the People's Republic to see relatives (a particularly shrewd move since it has led to so much Taiwanese investment in the ancestral homeland). It continues now with an elaborate and effective diplomatic offensive against what had once been, when Taiwan was comparatively poor, an indifferent world. Canada, along with Australia and New Zealand, has already (while ignoring mutterings from the People's Republic) opened direct air links with Taiwan and taken other such steps which the Taiwanese find promising. Italy, France, and most important of all, the new united Germany, have actually come round to full diplomatic relations. Much more activity of both kinds is expected to follow soon from other members of the European Community. Meanwhile, the Taiwanese have been quick off the mark (much quicker than Canadians, for example) to elbow their way into the new markets opening up in eastern Europe.

What does the KMT have in mind for the long term in order to keep all factions happy and to rejuvenate itself? Clearly some kind of sovereignty-association with the Mainland in which, unlike Hongkong, Taiwan would run its own political institutions and have a separate presence in the world while enjoying some type of relationship with the People's Republic that goes well beyond free trade but falls far short of surrender.

To make anything of this type happen, of course, Taiwan must continue to make lots of money. Fortunately, it has the knack.

The news in November that the Taiwanese are paying two billion American dollars for a forty-percent stake in McDonnell Douglas creates quite a sensation in the business world. It is taken as a signal that yet another important American industry—aerospace—will have to compete against Asians. This is a sign that the Taiwanese in particular have suddenly (to western eyes) come up in the world, to the point of posing a threat. Taiwanese dynamism should have been obvious long before. It's certainly obvious from within Taiwan, looking outward. In many societies, architectural landmarks and institutions recall past glories. In the Republic of China, which Taiwan has been for only one long generation, they instead tend to reflect present realities and future probabilities.

ℰℭ

The finest place to visit in Taipei is the National Palace Museum, which houses the world's most important collection of Chinese art and antiquities, including the former contents of the Forbidden City in Beijing. The collection has its origins in the Sung dynasty (960-1279), but the present building, in the Shihlin district on the north side of Taipei, dates only from 1965. Boyle Huang was the architect; he is now a Chinese-art consultant in Toronto.

The museum was long thought to house an extraordinary 700,000 items, but the official total keeps growing, thanks not only to purchases and donations but to a new inventory that is still in progress; at present the figure stands at 760,000. The most extensive holdings are in the areas of porcelain, ceramics, ritual bronzes, and painting and calligraphy, but the mandate extends to collections of jade, enamel ware, lacquerware, and rare books and manuscripts, which are all far more than simply representative.

Collecting began through the efforts of the Sung emperor T'ai-tzu and was carried on by his successors down through the centuries until artistic treasure filled the display rooms and storerooms of the capital. For most of this period, this was Beijing's Forbidden City, where none but members of the court and royal household ever saw the collection. That it was maintained throughout various wars and upheavals is little short of miraculous. With the collapse of the Qing dynasty in 1911, gathering came to an end, but the new Chinese republic opened the hoard to the public. After 1925, when P'u-yi, the last emperor, was banished, authorities began cataloguing the treasures and designated the spot where they were kept as the National Palace Museum. But that was only the beginning of the incredible story of the collection's survival.

When the Japanese invaded Manchuria in 1931, the collection was moved south to Shanghai for safe-keeping. Then it had to be moved again—this time to Nanjing. When the

Japanese occupation became an actual Sino-Japanese war in 1937, most of the objects were hidden in three widely scattered locations as far away as Sichuan, more than 1,600 kilometres up the Yangtze River. One lot of 7,000 crates was removed from a building in Hunan Province only one day before the site was destroyed. The last survivor of this heroic preservation effort is Na Chi-liang, now eighty-five. He lives rent free in a house at the rear of the museum grounds, a national hero.

The treasure had to remain hidden for years, as the Sino-Japanese conflict blended into the Second World War. After the peace in 1945, the government of Chiang Kai-shek reassembled all the old imperial collections in one place: Nanjing, the Nationalist capital. When, in a few years, it became clear that the communists under Mao Zedong might overrun Nanjing, most of the pieces, including all the choicest ones, were removed from the Mainland and taken offshore to Taiwan.

The pieces were kept in Taichung before facilities were ready in Taipei, where the Nationalists carried on business as the Republic of China. For its part, the People's Republic opened its own National Palace Museum in the now sparsely endowed Forbidden City (as well as establishing other new institutions, particularly the formidable Shanghai Museum of Art, which opened in 1952). Thus there came to be two National Palace Museums—unwitting symbols of the two governments, each of which claimed to be the legitimate government of China.

The Taipei museum is immense, with display areas and offices totalling 8,300 *p'ing* (27,870 square metres) and employing 600 people. Of course, only a small portion of the vast collections, between 7,000 and 9,000 items, can be shown at any one time. So there is a large permanent exhibit, "The Relationship Between Chinese and World Culture," on the ground floor, to give visitors an overview and provide a necessary foundation for the various other displays, such as paintings (changed every three months) or ceramics (changed every one to three years). There are naturally many famous works by individual artists and craftspeople: virtually all the greatest names in the history of Chinese calligraphy are represented, for instance. But I found, as I imagine many visitors do, that I came away with the most vivid memories of some of the smallest and least-touted objects.

But perhaps the site that people in the city most enjoy showing guests is the mammoth complex that comprises both the National Cultural Center and the Chiang Kai-shek Memorial Hall. It is imposing. It is meant to be.

The Cultural Center is an elaborate concert hall and an equally grand theatre famous as a venue for Taiwanese opera, which is more colourful, more gestural than the Mainland kind, with firecrackers at times and certainly a freer interpretation of the classic texts. Because not everyone speaks both

Mandarin and the Taiwanese dialect (called *Hokkien*), written characters are often projected down to the stage from the fourth balcony to help the audience along. Like all such subsidized palaces of art, this one reflects a kind of official charade. The real world of Taiwanese culture is a business, and as in all other Taiwanese businesses, the atmosphere is cutthroat. Even in the shadow of Hongkong's famous film industry, Taiwan made scores of feature films a year; it now makes only six or eight—and the big studio is more a tourist attraction than a place of creative enterprise. The Taiwanese can't compete against the Americans when it comes to visual trash. Conversely, the Mainland Chinese can't compete against the Taiwanese for the aural kind: Taiwanese rockers and pop singers (the most famous one is named Su Rui) are the stars of the People's Republic, thanks to radio signals that penetrate far beyond the coastal areas, to as far west as Sichuan.

The Memorial Hall, which opened in 1980 to mark the fifth anniversary of Chiang's passing, is covered in local marble and approached by means of a long avenue, flights of mammoth steps and a sixteen-metre-high bronze door weighing seventy-five tonnes, behind which is the message: *No entry for those wearing slippers or slovenly dress.* It is a monument to Chiang's personality rather than, strictly speaking, to his life. The exhibits relaying the biographical facts make no mention of, for example, the Green Circle, the criminal syndicate that ran

Shanghai in the 1920s and '30s and sheltered him when he needed help. This curatorial approach allows Chiang to be seen to be more flexible in death than he was in life, more like Lincoln in that respect than Mao, say. Two of his limousines are on exhibit, one of them a 1955 Cadillac with special bullet-proofing. A third limo is to be seen in Kaohsiung in the south. One begins to suspect that his automobiles are as numerous as Lenin's overcoats, or places where George Washington slept, or pieces of the True Cross.

The real monument to the Chiang legacy is the Grand Hotel, despite its age one of the fanciest and most famous in Asia (what the Taiwanese call a five-blossom hotel). It's built to resemble an enormous Chinese palace and sits atop a mountain called Round Hill, commanding a view of the city to the south. It was constructed by a group of investors led by Madame Chiang (who's still alive, in her nineties, living in seclusion in New York State—what a life she's had). But unlike, say, the Acropolis in Athens, the Grand can't usually be seen from the city down below: the buildings are so densely packed down there, and the smog so bad, that being in the Grand is like looking through a one-way mirror—you can see them, but they can't see you. The Grand, which boasts of having the largest classical Chinese roof in the world, is in two sections, an Old and a New, the former built back into the lush side of the mountain. That the whole place is huge—enormous imperial buildings linked with gardens and pathways—and yet has a combined total of only 575 guest rooms, gives some indication of how generous the suites are.

The Grand is a shrine to prosperity rather than to memory, and in modern Taiwan, that seems altogether appropriate. It overlooks all the other recent landmarks where money is made and managed. This is somehow appropriate, or at least symbolically correct.

Off in the distance, for example, is the tallest building in Taipei, the five-year-old World Trade Center, or rather the thirty-four-storey tower of the China External Trade Development Council, which, along with a hotel and an enormous convention centre, makes up the complex. The convention centre is booked with trade fairs from now until doomsday. When I pass through on my way to interview the head of CETDC, carpenters and gaffers descend on the scene like insects, striking the Taipei International Medical Equipment & Pharmaceuticals Show, replacing it with booths and displays for the Taipei Aerospace Technology Exhibit. Even more telling is the adjoining exhibition hall: six floors of small cubicles where thousands of Taiwanese manufacturers display their wares, from computers to gadgets and gimcracks. It's as though an invisible motto hangs over the place for the benefit of the 3,000 or so business people who come through every day: "Whatever you want, we'll make it cheaper." This is how Taiwan has come out of the blue to have the world's largest container fleet and, now that Japan is dumping dollars to prop up the yen, the world's largest foreign exchange surplus. Increasingly, though, manufacturing itself is being exported, a trend that must continue for a number of reasons.

One reason is concern for the environment. This is a matter Taiwanese politicians cannot afford to ignore, given the smog and the general ecological deterioration—and the ease with which they can score points abroad, as when the government recently agreed to ban drift net fishing. Another is the abiding search for ever cheaper labour. The People's Republic might seem a limitless resource in that respect, but the need to seek out the willing poor must to some extent be as much behind recent diplomatic overtures to places such as Vietnam as the need to create more markets by investing in them. These trends dovetail with Taiwan's inevitable wish that, as its economy grows, it will become more complex and sophisticated as well: that Taipei will become less a manufacturing centre and increasingly a financial one. There is reason to believe that this will happen. In the year just ended, one study put the shortage of capital in financial markets at about US$140 billion, of which Japan, the dominant force in Asia, could offer only about one-half. There's plenty of room for subsidiary centres in the region. That's why I hurry off to take a look at the Taipei Stock Exchange.

Such concrete institutions as the Taipei Stock Exchange (as distinct from abstract ones, such as the constitution) are already fully formed (which makes the West's astonishment about the Taiwanese economy itself all the more surprising). But the Exchange, though opened for business as long ago as 1962 as a sort of in-house kerb market, is only now beginning to take off. All the signs are present, including infantile volatility and a sense of go-goism that even Vancouver might envy.

At present, the recession has taken some of the shine off the figures but the atmosphere is still quite extraordinary. Part of the cause of the excitement, and some of its effect, was a ten-fold increase in the number of brokers at the very end of the 1980s and the start of the '90s, to the point where there are two reps for each listed company. The Taiwanese are *avid* for golf but they're *obsessed* with the stock market. In the period when the board was flashing like the flight-deck of a spaceship (the exchange uses the computer-assisted trading system developed by the Toronto Stock Exchange, with Japanese modifications), it was common for ordinary citizens to quit their well-paying jobs and spend all day at their brokers', transfixed by the spectacle. Towards the end of 1987, the Taipei index stood at 1,000. It had climbed to 12,000 by March 1989 when it promptly fell to 2,000, only to reach 12,000 again in February 1990. During my stay in Taipei the index stands at about 4,300. One day it jumps 127 points following news that a political demonstration on the independence issue did not end in violence as had been feared.

The Exchange itself, as a physical place, is not what's

interesting. Electronics have imposed a postmodern distance in such situations anyway, and nowhere else more than in Taipei. The growth in trading has caused the Exchange to be spread across the city in several different buildings, only one of which, the six-year-old data-processing centre, is purpose-built. The administrative offices, where I go for a briefing, are on six floors of a nondescript structure near City Hall and directly opposite police headquarters (a tall and somewhat scary edifice with an American-style eagle on the front and a heliport on top). The whole system has several revealing peculiarities. A board lot here is not a hundred shares but a thousand, as would be true in Canada only of junior resource stocks and other penny dreadfuls. And the market trades only from nine a.m. to noon (as well as from nine a.m. to eleven a.m. Saturdays). But the level of regulation this suggests is not apparent otherwise. Consider the fact that dealers, brokers, underwriters, bankers, and insurers can all be one and the same. Yet *deregulation* is not quite the correct term either, since there's little heritage of claustrophobic supervision to react against, except in terms of allowing foreign investment—and that's coming soon, as soon as it can be achieved with a degree of orderliness. Which is to say, as soon as it's politically safe to cut through the tangle of regulations prohibiting it now. In the meantime, the finance minister wants to see new flotations by the larger state-run companies—China Steel, China Ship-building, China Airlines, and the three largest commercial banks—to pump up volume and make manipulation more difficult. To that end, a new private bank is being established, and its shares, too, will be thrown into the pit. This is all according to the famous Six-Year Plan for national reconstruction.

None of the change is fast enough or dangerous enough to contain the citizens of Taiwan. Each business day, stocks traded on the Exchange have a total worth of somewhere between forty billion and ninety billion New Taiwan Dollars (NT$). But on some days, almost as much is traded on the unofficial and highly illegal underground exchange, and one Chinese-language business paper, the *Commercial Times*, has estimated that on occasion the underground action has reached NT$200 billion a day. Actually, the underground exchange isn't an exchange at all, as no shares change hands. It's more of a cross between a futures market and the numbers racket. People phone their bookie, er, broker, and lay bets on which way individual stocks, or the entire index, will move. Some of the biggest financial names on the island are involved in this activity. Some have gone to jail. The underground market has led to the creation of complete underground banks. One of them was discovered to have illegally accepted nearly NT$85 million in deposits. In all, fifty-eight of the bank's officials were convicted. Wonderful stuff.

Some on Taiwan contend that the people there are growing lazy, smug, and non-productive. One hears a great deal of anxious chatter about yuppies. Those local councils controlled by the DPP and other opposition parties have cut back the civil service work-week to five days. Now comes talk that the central government may permit its people to take off the final Saturday of each month. And in a few months there may be another national holiday for everyone: Children's Day, April 4. This would be tantamount to a spring break, since Tomb-Sweeping Day falls on April 5. As it stands, the Taiwanese celebrate seventeen national holidays, as compared with a mere eleven for Canadians. There is fear in some circles that the whole society is growing soft and flabby. The average Taiwanese works 45.5 hours a week. That's three and a half more than the average Japanese, but far behind the average South Korean, who works an incredible fifty-four hours. How can we hold up our heads, people say, when we're losing ground to the South Koreans? How indeed.

ꕥ

When Taiwan really began to boom economically about fifteen years ago, it expanded to the south and east. This was a matter of geography, but it was not without symbolic logic as well. As the northern part of Taiwan is better developed than the southern, so is the western more important than the eastern. Railways run up both sides of the island, for example, but the one on the west coast is electrified and that on the east coast, diesel. There are powerful historical reasons for this. The west coast, after all, faces the Chinese Mainland. It is also protected by the Central Mountain Range, which runs down the length of the island but slightly off-centre, giving the Strait side a much wider coastal bench than the Pacific side enjoys. In the *other* typhoon season, from April through August, the mountains help deflect the winds sweeping up from the southeast.

International air travel to and from Taipei, a matter of sub-diplomatic manoeuvring, is growing rapidly in response to bullish economic conditions, but flights within Taiwan are less of a priority: the weather is too unpredictable to permit strict schedules to be maintained. The main means of getting around is the Sun Yat-sen Freeway, a four-lane toll road, which on maps looks like the femoral artery on the island's anatomy. It begins at the top of the island, near Keelung, the second largest port for container shipping, and runs eighty percent of the way down, to Kaohsiung, the biggest such port, and fourth largest in the world. I am finally breaking free of Taipei and striking out through some of the countryside between the two termini. My slow, discontinuous circumnavigation of Taiwan is finally about to get underway in earnest.

The government has kindly laid on a car and driver. The former has two small ROC flags on the front, giving us the appearance of a one-unit diplomatic convoy; the latter speaks Taiwanese, very common in the south, which he uses rather than Mandarin when conversing with his countrymen there. I wear a security badge identifying me as a representative of the *Kingston Whig-Standard*. The people in the Government Information Office in Taipei had some difficulty translating the name of the newspaper into written Chinese; after consulting various English-language dictionaries and asking the advice of fluent anglophones, they came up with something like "flag of the independent anti-slavery democrats." Not a bad description, I say to myself.

The boom has made the middle class rich and created a new middle class from much of the rest, but poverty of course remains. You can see it as soon as you leave the city—people living in dark slum buildings with old discarded tyres atop the roof to hold the tar-paper or the rusty iron sheeting in place. But this is by no means Latin America or even the poorest parts of the People's Republic. In sizable cities along the way, your eye is naturally drawn to shop signs with pictures that tell you what sorts of businesses they are. I am struck by the number of commercial kennels advertising popular western breeds of dog, such as Dalmatians or terriers. Some people may still eat dog, especially as a winter delicacy, as in the People's Republic, but a vast, newly prosperous middle class has taken to owning pets in the western manner. One also sees a lot of restaurants with reversed swastikas painted on the front; this has nothing to do with Nazis but is an indication that the restaurant is run by Buddhists and is therefore vegetarian. One also sees many large reproductions of the Statue of Liberty, including a particularly huge one towering over yet another restaurant. These aren't signs of solidarity with the pro-democracy movement in the People's Republic, where the students erected such a statue in Tiananmen Square shortly before many were massacred; they are indications of the Taiwanese love of most things American. Personally, I find my first brush with a Statue of Liberty in Taiwan about as distasteful as my initial encounter with dog meat in a food stall in Beijing.

To mistake mere drabness for real poverty is easily done, especially in Chinese culture, where colours sometimes serve different functions than they do in the West. In Taipei, and in the small cities we keep passing through as we progress down the coast, government buildings are decorated with what looks like festive abandon: bright red, yellow, and blue banners are draped permanently across the tops, and the signage has an almost carnival connotation to foreigners who can't read the characters. By comparison, places of business, even the mammoth department stores found everywhere in coastal Asia, seem severely understated from the outside. And death too is every bit as colourful as government. Tooling down the highway we hear honking and loud Chinese music gaining on us from the other lane. The outside of the hearse is covered—sides, roof, bonnet, windows, wheels—with the brightest of flowers—not merely white for death but yellows, reds, greens. Following behind at a high rate of speed is a series of Japanese four-by-fours, similarly adorned, each containing a cluster of musicians in the open back, blowing on horns and woodwinds, loudly and with independence of spirit, pointing their instruments skyward, like soloists executing a difficult passage. Given all this, I've always found it hard to know how to interpret the squarish concrete low-rises and high-rises seen all over southeast Asia—grey, unpainted, with never enough windows and even those preternaturally small—buildings that always look old and used-up even when they're new. Whether residential or commercial, the style is the same, down to the corrugated steel rain barrels on the roof. In fact, it's frequently hard to tell at a short distance to what use such buildings are being put. This is the *other* traditional architecture of China, the one behind the red-tiled temples and the like. Can it really be as ubiquitous as it seems? Is it really as depressing as it looks?

Setting foot out of the capital is enough to tell you where all the merchandise displayed in the World Trade Center actually comes from: there are small factories everywhere, for every conceivable type of goods. It may not be quite true to say that the Republic practises manufacturing the way the People's Republic does agriculture: intensively, with every level square metre put to good use. But they each do what they do as though their lives depend on it (as indeed they do), and along the major transportation routes like this one the results are obvious: factory after factory. But as you move down the island, farming is apparent as well, particularly the big cash crops such as sugar cane and corn and betel nuts. The last of these the rural Taiwanese chew addictively, despite government health warnings that the habit may cause cancer. At lunch time, we stop to get some ears of corn, boiled on the spot in a vessel made from a metal drum. The kernels are ivory in colour and twice as large as the variety we're most familiar with at home. They are delicious.

The high mountains appear unbroken in the distance. Very Chinese mountains they seem, too, in the way the summits dip down and swing back up the ends, like the roofs of palaces all in a row. But near Changhua on the Tatu River we leave the big dual carriageway and swing inland, heading for Sun Moon Lake, a famous scenic wonder high up in the Central Range, just about dead centre on a map of the island. As we climb higher and higher, the mountains begin to take on a different character: not jagged, sloping peaks in choreographed sequence but huge obstinate loaves, a thousand metres tall perhaps, densely forested, and standing closely together, each blocking the view of the next.

Sun Moon Lake, 760 metres up a long switchbacking road, is a place of considerable loveliness and even more tranquility. The water is a delicate blue, with jade-like streaks of green along the margins. At its bluest, it looks like the glaze used in Ching porcelain. Its elevation, its calmness, its apparent remoteness from the world all call to mind Windermere in the

Lake District, but Sun Moon Lake is far larger. There's an island sitting in it where Chiang Kai-shek had a holiday home (as cottages are called in Taiwan). I walk round the shore for a bit and find a spring percolating madly in a little inlet. This is the source of supply for the entire lake. Tall bamboo and giant ferns flourish near the shore. Other less delicate flora dominate the farther up you climb.

On the crest of the lake is a large temple, not as intrinsically interesting, I think, as one I saw earlier at Tanshui, where a golden Buddha with twenty-one hands is approached by tunnels bored through a mountain. The lakeside shrine is called the Hsuanchuang Temple—the Temple of Literature and Power, a reference to the scholars of the ancient court who wielded administrative authority only by working harmoniously with the military. The real man-made attraction of Sun Moon Lake is the nine-storey Tzuen Pagoda, built about thirty years ago at the very top of one of the encircling mountains.

I can see that the morning fog is going to obstruct what people tell me is the magnificent 360-degree view, but we trudge up nonetheless, simply to get a look at the pagoda itself. The long tough climb exhausts many visitors, I am told. Among the dense foliage along the way are occasional papaya trees; the fruit is ripe at this time of year, and Filipino tourists, seeing its yellow, are reminded of a pun involving a "red joke"—a blue joke, we would say. Poinsettias, which

Taiwanese Christians regard the same way western Christians do, as a Christmas plant, grow wild along the path. The pagoda is indeed a restful spot—and a rest is what's needed once you've gone round nine circular flights of stairs. The fog, which seems to touch the shore at certain points and then pull back, like a blind person navigating among unfamiliar obstacles, makes the scene all the more relaxing. We linger a while.

An enormous bronze bell hangs from a stout beam at the top of the pagoda. On close inspection we find that it carries the Taiwanese flag, not religious symbols, as its motif. Back down below, near the car park, there are shops selling large fungi, native crafts, and butane cigarette lighters with pictures of naked women on them. This is an unsubtle reminder of a more important fact: that Taiwan is not only far more westernized than the People's Republic but far more traditional, too, in some ways. After all, it hasn't had a Cultural Revolution and years of indoctrination camps to erase folkways and old beliefs. In any case, the incongruity of the selection strikes me because it seems to say a lot about how Taiwan looks at itself and its place in the world.

As if to prosecute the point, a short distance away is the Formosan Aboriginal Culture Village.

There are ten aboriginal tribes in Taiwan: the Ami, Atayal, Bunum, Paiwan, Puyuma, Rukai, Shao, Saisiat, Tsou, and Yami. All are quite different, and they are spread out across the island and offshore. One of the tribes is found on Lanyü in the Pacific, but most lived originally on the Strait, where for years one tribe preyed on Chinese and European shipwreck victims. Still another practised a religion that involved use of their enemies' severed heads—a fact alluded to in the preservation of the ceremonial stone shelving where the heads were once kept, row on row. All had complex cultures long before the Chinese arrived in force. Their continued existence, both in their natural habitat in the mountains and here, as a tourist draw, speaks well for their resilience; the pressure to come down into the cities and marry Chinese is stronger every year. The village, however, does not give much hint of their political importance. Aboriginals have no special status, like Natives in Canada, but they have taken an important part in the movement for direct democracy and all that entails.

The tragedy of the Formosan Aboriginal Culture Village is its entertainment value. There is a stage where members of the tribes put on a joint musical and theatrical performance, a kind of slick pastiche of the ten traditions. For domestic rather than western tourists, there is also an enormous restaurant made to look like an eighteenth-century French stately home, complete with vast formal gardens in the European manner. Soon, so goes the rumour in business circles, some Disney or at least Disneyesque theme park is to be built adjacent to this. Conversely, the value of the village is the way in which it brings together in one place some indication of the ten tribes. Learning here is much easier than learning by tracking down separate sites in all thirteen counties. The village consists of examples of the various types of dwelling used by the aboriginals. They are as different as a thatched hut and a stout house of flat stones piled up without mortar, resembling a structure you would expect to see in the Orkneys. Much of what's on display in the village no longer exists in the wild but is preserved or reconstructed from field research done as long ago as the 1930s.

There is also an adequate museum, and examples of aboriginal carving everywhere, including much that is phallic in nature. An interesting difference this: in the People's Republic, the aboriginals would have been at least forcibly assimilated by the communists and probably persecuted quite rigorously, with the government all the while eulogizing them as special. In Taiwan, they are genuinely protected, even nurtured, but the nurturing takes such a commercial form as to be destructive in its own way. On the one side of the Strait, all action regardless of the motive tends towards struggle and opposition; on the other, all action tends towards business. This is not a cultural stereotype ("Irrepressible entrepreneurs, those Taiwanese"). It's a national trait incorporated into Taiwanese society as necessary for survival. As the aboriginals have learned to sing and dance for the tourists in order to earn the privilege of being left alone the rest of the time, so the Taiwanese have learned to make money in the most competitive markets in the world in order to go on enjoying being Taiwanese.

We have to put up for the night at Taichung, as almost everyone who's been in the mountains must do. Although it is Taiwan's third-biggest city, after Taipei and Kaohsiung, it's a very distant third indeed. No cosmopolitanism here, just a sense of being in some inland provincial place that has grown faster than its ability to metabolize change: a sense the traveller experiences more often on the Mainland. We stay in a nondescript tourist hotel and when we go to dinner we find we are practically the only people in the ballroom-sized restaurant, which nonetheless must have twelve to fifteen waiters on duty. We pack up at first light, as the old people are starting to gather in the park for their tai chi. Also, the first few students are making a reluctant appearance: young girls in burgundy blazers, carrying their school books in leather straps slung over their shoulders.

If the northern one-third of the island is conspicuous for light industry, the middle third, from Taichung down to Tainan, is much more agricultural. There are rice paddies stretching on forever and fish-farms in neat artificial lakes making mosaic patterns on the landscape. Poultry is important as well. From a certain distance the masses of ducks waddling across the scenery look like white flowers waving in the wind. In this area, the mountains are no longer visible from the highway.

In less than a couple of hours you come to Tainan, the old capital of Taiwan (until 1885) and the city with the most spiritual significance: the Kyoto to Taipei's Tokyo, as it were. Mind you, this part of its character is not always apparent at first look. But in the alleys off the main streets and the lanes off the alleys, scores and scores of temples, Confucian and Taoist, sit hidden—churches, too, for Tainan is the most Christianized place in the Republic of China, with the baptized population exceeding ten percent of the whole, according to one guide book. At least two of the more important temples date to the seventeenth century. They hint at the wave of religious and cultural reclamation following Koxinga's defeat of the Dutch East India Company traders—of whom, by contrast, almost no reminders survive.

When Koxinga captured Casteel Zeelandia, he built his own stronghold atop it and named the result Fort Anping. (Six months later, he was dead at the age of thirty-seven or thirty-eight.) Nearly all of Fort Anping was destroyed in the nineteenth century in what must have been a formidable typhoon indeed. By that time, the site, once right on the water, was rapidly becoming an inland one, as the harbour silted up. It is now not only dry but in the middle of a very urban area.

The reconstructed buildings that mark the spot today don't ask much of one's imagination, though on climbing to the top of a little blockhouse to look down on some old Chinese cannon with long carriages, I am delighted to see the semicircular foundation of one of the Dutch towers still visible down below. Its origins are unmistakable, being made of the thin yellowish bricks called *klompje baksteen*. In this instance, the bricks had been brought from Batavia.

A short distance away is Yitszi Chin Cheng, a small moated fort built by French engineers in the 1870s when the Ching dynasty was worried, prematurely as it happened, about Japanese designs on Taiwan (a name, incidentally, first applied only to the Tainan area, before the rest of Formosa was developed). Yitszi Chin Cheng is an earthen fort with a traditional Chinese gate, boasting enormous old shore gun batteries built by Armstrong. Like some others, supplied by Krupp, which have since disappeared, they were in their day the last word in prestigious European death technology. School children play on the guns now. How often old forts turn out to be peaceful, contemplative places—more so sometimes than many of the temples.

Tainan seems a world away from the heavy industrial sector in the south, whose nerve centre is Kaohsiung, long familiar to anyone involved in Pacific shipping (or anyone who likes to read about it) but now growing beyond its origins without actually outgrowing them. You see the industrial landscape changing kilometre after kilometre as you move towards the city. Agriculture gets smaller and smaller in scale, factories bigger and closer together. On the afternoon we are driving past, I fancy that we can tell the exact spot where the two worlds come together. A man and a boy in a conical straw hat are fishing with wispy bamboo poles. Their stream is a concrete culvert running alongside a refinery. Behind them in the distance a big red sign flashes letters one at a time—*T-O-Y-O-T-A*—followed by the complete word, *TOYOTA*, in endless alternation.

So it is a surprise to get into central Kaohsiung and find it so pleasant-looking—much more handsome than Taipei and more orderly as well. Like a just-bought shirt still stiff with sizing and full of pins, the major buildings haven't lost their newness yet. But neither have they completely usurped the old low wooden structures of the past, which can be found not only on side streets and alleys but sometimes, in twos or threes, on the leafy thoroughfares as well. The city is bisected by the Love River, and the traffic bounces over the bridges in a multi- coloured parade. The city and harbour sit in a kind of broad basin, with mountains in the middle distance most of the way around. Some of the mountains are green but others have bare terraces in stripes round the top, the work of the cement industry thereabouts.

Environmental concerns are worrisome throughout Taiwan, and with reason. After all, it's a small island—six hours by car from top to bottom if conditions are right—and in only a few years it has gone from near insignificance financially to being the world's twelfth-largest economy. Such transitions exact a big price, but the politicians are determined that their cities won't become like Bangkok. To judge by the press, television, and what I get from fifty-odd conversations around the island, the environment is a more frequent topic of public discourse than it is in the United States, say. The lifting of martial law, under which all public demonstrations were banned, has doubtless increased the concern by providing outlets for pent-up anxiety. Not that long ago, persistent protests actually forced China Petroleum to cancel, or at least postpone, construction of another refinery in the city.

The saddest fact about Kaohsiung is that it is home to what is probably the world's largest scrapyard for ocean-going vessels: a heartbreaking place for people who love ships. Seeing it is almost enough to make you swear off air travel if you could, as a visit to a slaughterhouse is the surest path to vegetarianism. At least the yard has recently been moved a few kilometres out of sight, and no longer destroys the mood of Kaohsiung Harbour, which is definitely upbeat. In Kaohsiung, all the personal luxuries both commonplace and exotic come from the profits of exporting. To understand what makes the place tick, you must plunge into this very competitive world of contracts and cargoes.

Cities like this in Taiwan and South Korea have taken over from places like Hamilton, Ontario, Pittsburgh, and Sheffield. Steel-making is not a protected industry in Taiwan. It's quite *laissez-faire*, though China Steel Corporation, the biggest of the 300 mills on the island, is also the only one owned by the state, which takes back ninety-eight percent of the extraordinarily high after-tax profit (of late, between twenty-five and thirty percent on sales). The China Steel facility is also the country's only integrated works, meaning that it imports the coal, coke, iron ore, and limestone it uses to feed its three blast furnaces rather than buying ingots ready made. The company employs about 10,000 people in total.

To North American eyes, some of the business practices seem rather Japanese. China Steel Corporation has a gym, a library, tennis courts, a post office, etc., for the workers, even a contemplation pond, made from one of the slag-heaps and stocked with goldfish (a second generation of them now). A dormitory capable of housing a thousand unmarried workers charges only about US$20 a month. The steel-making process is much more up to date than you might expect, given that the mills look very much like our own. Escaping heat from the furnaces (1,040 degrees Fahrenheit) is captured and directed to other purposes; there's little smoke emitted from the stacks and what there is, having passed through an elaborate filtering system, is white, not black. The site takes up 220 hectares. As late as 1971, the land was still a cane brake.

Next door, at one of the two yards of China Shipbuilding Corporation, the story is the same. In 1974, this was a fish pond. It's now 120 hectares of immense drydocks and plate-shops. So far, it has repaired, refitted, or jumboized 1,600 ships and designed and built 262 others—tankers, bulk carries, container ships, passenger ships, and small naval vessels, such as patrol boats like the one I see but am forbidden to photograph. The yard also turns out offshore oil rigs and is licensed to make nuclear power-plant components. The competition is keen, the clientele world wide. This is where most of Taiwan's own fleet has originated—the result of competitiveness moreso than patronage.

"See that?" asks the official who shows me around, pointing to a nearly completed container ship of the local Yang Ming Line. "Two hundred and seventy metres long. Costs $60 million. Very cheap." His tone is that of a dealer in stereo equipment.

China Steel has a fleet of four ore carriers, bringing in raw material from Australia, Malaysia, and Canada. The hull plates were made in their own continuous-rolling mills and the vessels designed and constructed by China Shipbuilding just over the fence.

"Everything was done according to tender," a China Steel rep tells me. "Very, very above-board all the way." By an eerie coincidence, the rep of China Shipbuilding uses almost identical language.

On a small peninsula across the harbour from these two giants is the Kaohsiung Export Processing Zone, one of three special industrial parks in Taiwan where manufacturers can bring in raw materials and components without duty if they process them on the spot and send the results directly overseas. The other two are at Keelung, on the northern tip of the island, and near Taichung. The Taichung site is given over completely to computers, semi-conductors, and the like, of which Taiwan has become a significant supplier. At twenty-five the eldest of the three, the Kaohsiung zone is also the one with the greatest diversity of tenants. Some small electronics companies are there but other firms in the complex make appliances, toys, clothing, or sporting goods. A duty-free shop for foreigners looks like one of those shops in the former Soviet Union where overseas visitors with hard currency could purchase luxury goods. The quality and range is depressingly about the same; there's simply not the breadth of design and cleverness here that you see displayed so well at the World Trade Center in Taipei. As an instrument of economic policy, however, the zone has certainly done its job in contributing to Taiwan's almost embarrassingly favourable balance of payments.

Some of the companies in the zone lease their factories from the government, while others have chosen to buy the land and erect their own buildings. The whole place covers eighty-six hectares and employs an astounding 22,000 workers. Significantly, though, eighty percent of them are girls of junior high-school age. This is not a place to create high-paying jobs for the populace; it's a place to make money for the entrepreneurs wishing to take advantage of what is still, by western if not by Asian standards, very cheap labour. At the shipyard across the way, boys as young as fifteen work nine hours a day for three years while going to class at night as they finish high school. The Taiwanese miracle is not being achieved without a price. As I return to Taipei to depart for Canada, I fancy that I can foresee the social unrest that this system must inevitably create.

1995

Those who follow these questions say that the two international airlines with the most stylish and punctilious in-flight service are Singapore Airlines and one of its newest rivals, Mandarin, which is owned by the government of the Republic of China. As I intend to avoid going to Singapore, an authoritarian state so strict that some believe people are hanged there for not rewinding video tapes before returning them, I have not flown on the former. But rumours about Mandarin turn out to be true. The food is superior, the level of comfort makes you feel guilty, and the flight attendants go so far as to memorize the names of all of the passengers. Such attention to detail is all to the good as I am on a twelve-hour non-stop flight from Vancouver. There are *three* full-length movies—two from Hollywood and one from China. There are also Japanese and Taiwanese videos. The Japanese ones are expensively produced and try, without success, to achieve a hint of MTV nihilism; one group actually called American Boyz turns out to be four Japanese youths who recall the innocent shenanigans of the Monkees. By contrast, Taiwanese videos all seem dreamily romantic, full of young women with bed-room eyes and yet full of anguish too. Perhaps they're performing ballads. It's difficult for me to know as I have the headset tuned to classical music. I'm delighted at how well the music seems to suit the action up on the screen, no matter what it is. After the triple feature, for instance, come some documentaries, including one about Antarctica. I marvel at how perfectly Brahms' dramatic flourishes synchronize with the crumbling of the ice shelf, how his lighter moments mock the silly strut of the penguins.

I know I am flying straight into a bureaucratic bramble in a few more hours' time. I have been eager to return to Taiwan to finish the circuit tour of the island that I began in 1991, and to see if the accelerated pace of development and investment has brought Taiwan any closer to its goal, so seemingly quixotic, of getting the world to recognize theirs as *the* government of China. Members of the Taiwanese foreign service are rotated to new postings every three years, so I had already been dealing with two succeeding representatives of the so-called Taipei Economic and Cultural Office in Toronto—part of a vast lobby and propaganda infrastructure poised to turn itself into a chain of diplomatic missions at a moment's notice. With the present one, C.I. Lai, a good-humoured former teacher turned PR type, about my own age, long conversations and longer lunches had taken place in which I made my case for visiting the parts of the country I hadn't seen. They were countered by the suggestion that I submit to formal interviews with minor government officials. Such stuff might fill the papers in Taiwan. But I would be hard put to find a Canadian magazine or newspaper willing to publish an exclusive one-on-one with Prime Minister Lee Teng-hui, much less some third- or fourth-rank cog in, say, the Industrial Development Bureau in the Council for Economic Planning and Development. It's travel- writing—descriptive travel-writing, adding up to some kind of current snapshot of the island—that my editors want to print. I thought I had finally got through to the GIO bureaucrats in Taipei. But as I am about to depart Vancouver I get a fax of my schedule and itinerary. It is heavy with interviews with civil servants and with trips to the tourist sites already too familiar to me from 1991—familiar to the world of travel-writing and travel-reading in general.

I arrive at Chiang Kai-shek Airport (or, as they now call it, Taipei Chiang Kai-shek Airport, to add just a little more distance between themselves and the wily old bandit) on April 4. This is the twentieth anniversary of Chiang's death, which this year coincides with Tomb-Sweeping Day, when families pay tribute to the departed by placing fruit and other goods at their graves and burning paper tributes. Observance of both these holidays is down dramatically in recent years, particularly among the young, but there is a holiday feel in the air nonetheless: the big spring vacation has just come to an end and people are returning to school or work after one of the few sustained absences permitted by the calendar.

At Arrivals, a young man in a plaid sports coat steps out of the crowd like a tentative assassin and calls my name. He gives me his card: Wei-Kwang Hao, Protocol Officer. "But you may call me Comrade," he says. This strikes me as an unusual request, especially in Taiwan of all places, but I'm prepared to go along with it. Comrade Hao whisks me out of the long Customs queue and sends me through the hard-to-find wicket where diplomats are allowed to bypass the usual formalities. Feeling that there's no time like the present, I tell him about my Vancouver fax and make polite suggestions about how my itinerary will have to be revised if what is after all the stated purpose of the journey is to be achieved. He slips back into the seat of the Mercedes that will take us in and out of thick traffic, past factories, factories everywhere. Our destination is the Grand Hotel, the ersatz temple—a temple of luxury, certainly—that still sits atop Yuan Shan (Round Hill) overlooking the Keelung River down below and the entire city beyond. I have evidently been bumped up to the Taiwanese A-list.

I sense that my comrade has had problems with itineraries before. He says he will see what he can do. We will meet in the morning before 0830. It's now—well, I'm not even sure which day it is, as the International Date Line has always confused me. But I am happy to be at the Grand, which was once highly recommended to me by someone whose name is worth dropping but which I've forgotten. (Next day: I believe it might have been Margaret Drabble.) Anyway, the Grand, which was built about forty years ago, never seems to make it into the rankings of the world's best hotels as compiled annually, with Academy Award-like ballyhoo, by the New York business magazine *Institutional Investor*. But clearly it belongs, and no doubt the Taiwanese take this as yet another slur on their claim to true nationhood. There is nothing of the chain or group aesthetic here. No Hilton, no Four Seasons. This is absolutely a one-off hotel, inspired architecturally by the Forbidden City in Beijing and suggesting some quality you might expect to find at the Raffles in dreaded Singapore but wouldn't have thought possible to have been built from scratch as recently as the 1950s. The Grand is renowned for the way it harmonizes western and Chinese furniture and decorative works. I am given one enormous and somewhat sparse room—of how many *p'ing* I cannot calculate. The floor is teak and shows the marks of the craftsman's adze. On the nightstand there is a card stating that a blind masseuse is available by pushing 5 on the phone. Being in a hotel such as this, one so huge it never gives any hint of being packed to capacity no matter what the occupancy rate, is like being on an ocean-liner that never goes anywhere. At three a.m. local time I'm wide awake and dressed, sitting on the balcony, watching distant traffic twinkle in the darkness. In three hours, a room service waiter will arrive with congee, a breakfast porridge that, I'm sorry to say, I've never mastered the art of keeping down. The morning will burn away the darkness and the smog for which Taipei is justly famous will take over.

The Taiwanese like to claim that they're the true preservers of traditional Chinese civilization. They like to remind you that they had no Mao to pull down the monasteries and the temples and the old city walls (even Beijing's). They didn't have to live through a period in which the practice of traditional arts and crafts was persecuted as a matter of politics. But it's also true that neither did the People's Republic take to the market economy with anything resembling the vigour of the Taiwanese (and then not until the 1970s and with increasing tempo only in the past five years), whose concern is always with the present, or future, and interminable advancement—a factor you see reflected in the literature of the younger generation. In the People's Republic, particularly out in the countryside, travellers will sometimes come across scenes that seem misplaced in time—a water buffalo pulling a plough in a field, for example. In Taiwan—certainly in urban Taiwan, which is mostly what I have seen so far—I get the eerie feeling that I am in the middle of some anachronism I cannot recognize. Until it hits me: the Taiwanese are like U.S. Republicans of the sort now extinct in the United States itself. They couldn't be less like such extremists as Ronald Reagan or Newt Gingrich. But with their golf shirts and business suits and increasingly sophisticated near-constant deal-making

—with, most important of all, their absolute commitment to orderly, moderate reform—they're like 1950s Republicans, Buick-driving country club Republicans, Nelson Rockefeller moderate Republicans: a breed that has survived here in Galapagos-like offshore isolation while the American models, with their chrome tail-fins and large dinosaur teeth, have disappeared from the Earth forever, recalled now only dimly as the butt of *New Yorker* cartoons.

Comrade Hao tells me a little about himself. He's in his late twenties, married, commutes three hours a day between the GIO office downtown and his high-rise apartment in a northern suburb.

"Usually, I escort the German-speaking guests," he explains, telling me that he studied in Germany for three years. "But so many people at the office have the flu that's going around that the English protocol officers are sick and I've had to take over your file even though English is my third language." As he speaks I realize that Comrade Hao's name is not Comrade. Most English-speaking Taiwanese take an English name for convenience when dealing with foreigners—Michael Wang or Helen Chung, say. My escort, being a German specialist, has taken a German one. His name of course is *Konrad.*

Which I commence to call him, working his name into every sentence, like some annoying Dale Carnegie-trained used car salesman, hoping to make up for earlier misunderstanding.

I lose my first round with the GIO bureaucracy, as Konrad,

after a series of long and complicated negotiations with his superiors, reports that we must adhere to the schedule for the first three days, so that he will then have a trade-off to offer in rearranging the remainder of the trip. But as it happens I win on points, as the bureaucracy, which is normally so well lubricated, starts to go awry.

Many Taiwanese are said to make a fetish of precision in arranging meetings. Konrad is to pick me up out front not at 8:15 or 8:30, but 8:20 exactly. Rain is coming down like a bed of nails, making a deafening racket on the upswept temple roof of the hotel. Visibility is very poor. The tropical foliage in the surrounding hills has blurred into a runny wash of dark green. The landscape seems to be running a fever. Although CKS Airport is not far away and one can hear the jets arriving and departing, no trace of them can be seen: Taipei must be a pilot's nightmare.

Following strict custom (as agreed on by host and guest countries), our first meeting is with the director of the so-called Canadian Trade Office, which is really the embassy-in-waiting, pending the day, not expected any time soon, when the two countries will resume normal diplomatic relations (over the dead body of the People's Republic). The agency shares a floor with the Toronto-Dominion Bank and other Canadian companies in a building in Fu Suing Road, and it resembles every other small Canadian consular outpost on the Foreign Affairs map: the boring statistical publications strewn about the waiting room, the rather tacky Group of Seven print (though in this case of J.E.H. MacDonald's "Supply Boat") in the adjoining boardroom. Typically, the GIO and the CTO have not been interfacing properly (perhaps the weather causes atmospheric disturbances) and so none of the Canadians knows I am coming nor does anyone understand who I am when I get there. I escape with a few questions addressed to an assistant, twenty-nine or thirty I would judge, wearing a nicely tailored suit of the boxy style and speaking in macros while sizing up his interlocutor. Foreign Affairs is still full of these people. As the Toronto police once recruited new cops by going into the Gorbals of Glasgow and holding up slabs of raw meat with which to incite entire street gangs into signing up, so someone at the Lester B. Pearson Building on Sussex Drive must continue to lurk in the ivy at McGill and Queen's, tugging on the sleeves of upper-middle-class WASP kids, promising them lives of exotic adventure.

I am on a roll of good luck, for at my first scheduled chat, the victim, the Director of the Sixth Division of the Industrial Development Bureau in the Ministry of Economic Affairs, is unavoidably detained, and the one after that—with the equally imposing title Executive Director of the Coordination and Service Office for the Asia-Pacific Regional Operations Center in the Council for Economic Policy and Development—has just left on his honeymoon (an embarrassed underling explains).

Being stood up saves a lot of precious time, as I know, from my reading and my visit here in 1991, what they would have said. After the usual ritual of slick pamphlets, and boiling water in paper cups, they would have explained how Taiwan has developed a systematic plan for becoming a more important "regional operations center" once the People's Republic reclaims most of Hongkong from the British in 1997 and Macao from the Portuguese in 1999. They would have explained, with graphics and audio-visuals, how the island will spend billions to establish itself as a central place in east Asia for making and selling value-added products. Methods will include building up the port facilities at Kaohsiung and elsewhere and putting an entirely new airport around the present airfield in Taipei. There will be a dramatic upgrade in telecommunications, media, and financial markets. The government sees Taiwan emerging after the death of Deng Xiaoping in Mainland China as a place where—for all its problems caused by wealth—democracy and human rights will grow apace with innovation in the market. Virtually all of east Asia has shown that the two sets of concerns are not exactly inseparable; Beijing and Singapore actually find them to be mutually exclusive. The Taiwanese have no particular ideological stake in their position; it seems to them simply that the one makes more sense than the other. They are, after all, admirers of a more liberal kind of capitalism that in the United States has faded into history. The U.S. has become more like the intransigent-fortress Taiwan of Chiang Kai-shek's day, while Taiwan, for its part, looks forward with vigour to the America of the 1950s. Of the Taiwanese, this might truly be said: They Like Ike.

Freed early of my obligations, I put on stout walking shoes and set out to reacquaint myself with Taipei City (as the natives call it to avoid confusion with Taipei County). It seems busier, more congested and dirtier than ever, more itself than ever before. Obviously, the city makes some attempts at planning, but they seem pretty superficial. For example, in trying to preserve or reinstate the city's claim to continuity, many of the old traditional businesses, such as herbalists' shops and dealers in paper-goods burned as offerings to the dead, have been brought together in a place called Chiu Street—Old Street. But many areas owe their distinctiveness to some other, more organic logic. There are two red-light districts, one American, the other Japanese. The former is called the Combat Zone, no doubt after the one in Boston (the Taiwanese love American names). With the same love of compartmentalizing, there is a distinct residential area for foreigners. Yet everything in Taipei—the financial district, the hotel row, the streets of department stores—seems to have taken shape without much overall forethought. Now that protest demonstrations are allowed, two of the most common varieties are those championing the quickly rising women's movement and those condemning poor, sub-substandard or overpriced construction. Taipei has wide boulevards, and narrow pavements, like most big Asian cities, but the former have been ruined and the latter made impassable by overhead freeways beneath which, in a wonderful use of space, outdoor markets take shape, particularly on weekends and holidays—one for books, another for jade, a third for flowers, and so on. Similarly, there is a beautiful utilitarian symmetry, but it is not obvious to the person merely passing through. In Taipei, the dawn is often a burnt orange—smog of a kind that stings the eyes and shakes the lungs—while the nightlife tends towards karaoke bars and their newer video equivalents, KTVs. (Hell, I believe, must be very much like Heaven, but with a Karaoke Nite.) In Taiwan, there is no regulation of real estate agents. All one needs to begin buying and selling is a business card. This seems to me indicative of a larger attitude.

All of which is to say that in the four years since my first visit, Taipei has become even more like it was. Yet I am never without the sense—no one could possibly be without the sense—that life here is getting better fast. A difficult realization to fully digest when you come from one of the cultures where things are only getting steadily worse.

Before liberalization in the late 1980s, in the days of martial law, Taiwan had thirty newspapers. With the end of government strictures, the number climbed to 300. Clearly there had to be a shake-out. But even now there are over 200 newspapers, including two with daily circulations of one million each and ten with more than 100,000 apiece—followed by a ragtag cacophony of little newspapers espousing every possible view-point about everything. Similarly, there are 100 radio stations, one-tenth of them government-controlled, and twice as many illegal pirate stations. When I was last here there were three TV channels, all with some degree of government participation (new rules limit government equity to forty percent). But there's now something called the Fourth Channel, which is no channel at all in our sense of the word but a strange shouting match between cable operations from the U.S., Hongkong, and elsewhere. Rupert Murdoch has his hand in, with a combination of cricket matches and American movies; so, even more inevitably, does Ted Turner. Or take health care. In an age when America is callously refusing to embrace universal health care, Britain is trying desperately to preserve some of its once admirable system, and Canada is losing ground every day, Taiwan has simply started up one from scratch (though not without howls from the opposition DPP and others). The scheme covers the entire population and has been in effect only about a month at the time of my visit. Only an economy that is expanding with head-spinning speed could attempt such a feat in today's environment.

Let me make my prejudices clear. Taiwan's Americanism makes me edgy (I'm a BBC World Service and not a CNN International sort of person), and I don't imbue democracy with great sentimental value in and of itself (who wouldn't prefer a benevolent monarch to an endless succession of elected despots?). Yet it's hard not to be heartened by what's going on here. The Kuomintang is still in power (and you see how it holds onto the reins by shifting left or right as necessary). But since my previous visit a new opposition party, called the New Party, composed of foreign-educated Young Turks, has come to prominence, provoking the old guard towards further liberalization, while the Democratic Progressives have taken the most important municipal and county seats of power. Early in 1996, Taiwan will for the first time elect a president by popular vote. All this new freedom comes because new riches have brought new attitudes, especially among the young, which is just the opposite of the effects of economic liberalization in most of the rest of Asia, where prosperity had been purchased at the price of human rights—especially, and most noticeably, in the Republic of China's motherland and adversary across the Strait.

$$\infty\text{G}$$

When I began my journey around Taiwan in 1991, the Taiwanese were not permitted to invest in Mainland China directly, but through Taiwanese subsidiary companies in Hongkong or Singapore they already owned over 3,000 factories and other businesses in the People's Republic (a name, by the way, that a ranking Kuomintang official used publicly for the first time the week of my return—a long-awaited and carefully planned slip of the tongue that made all the front pages). Most of these factories were in the nearest parts of the People's Republic, the provinces of Fujien and Guangdong, where many Taiwanese have family ties. Now, only four years later, the official Taiwanese count is 11,000 Taiwan-owned factories spread out in all but one or two of Mainland China's provinces and so-called autonomous zones, from Sichuan and even Tibet in the far west to Manchuria in the north. Radio broadcasts monitored from Mainland China put the figure much higher—20,000 factories as of last year, worth an estimated US$20 billion. Seeking clarification, Taiwan's economic affairs ministry retained an academic think-tank to find out the true figure; the report came back endorsing Beijing's estimates as accurate.

Many of these factories dot the old lines of European colonialism. A Taiwan company in one of the four big fields (electronics, shoes, plastics, metal processing) might decide to set up a branch of its Shanghai operation upriver in Wuhan, for instance. "In the future," an official at the Mainland Affairs Council tells me, "these growth rates will decline, because Mainland China has brought in new labour laws and pollution controls." Also, competition among the Taiwanese themselves is hurting everyone. Mind you, the growth will still be fast by objective standards. Even now, wages in Taiwan are ten to fifteen times higher than on the Mainland. What's more, the family connection has made the Taiwanese more successful than anyone else at penetrating the domestic Mainland market—not just on the coast but far up-country: a prize that has so far eluded envious Japanese, Europeans, and Americans. "It may be that in five years' time," my informant continues, "after Mr Deng has died and also after we see how the Hongkong problem is settled, we will see another big boom" in Taiwanese investment. Now it's centred on small businesses, employing 500, 750, or even 2,000. But Taiwan's majors, such as the great petrochemical companies and motorcycle manufacturers, are ready to move in once they have some assurance that the market is safe, once they can devise some clear notion of what the future relationship between the two Chinas will be. This is why next spring's presidential election will be followed so closely. The Kuomintang platform is for unification without two separate countries—that is, doing through economic means what Chiang had not the slightest chance of doing militarily: retaking the Mainland. Conversely, the New Party promises simple "unification" and the Democratic Progressives of course want to declare a new republic, independent not only of Mainland China but of its old self, with the endless wrangling that has gone along with it. The attention of China-watchers will be unusually rapt.

One day Konrad has to bring his son along because the boy's kindergarten has been cancelled due to the epidemics of flu and viral pneumonia. The lad is five years old. Like so many Chinese kids he is impossibly cute and wears what looks like the Beatles' original 1964 haircut. He also has a dreadful chest cold and is coughing incessantly in the air-conditioned car. "Young ones get sick very easily in Taipei because of the pollution," his father explains. Sure enough I catch the boy's ailment by the next morning, when I wake up voiceless and with a racking cough and a big lumpy immovable congestion sitting in my lungs like a ball of unbaked dough. I decide that my best course might be a sauna to dry out my innards.

Sauna and massage customs present much to interest the sociologist and anthropologist, as they still seem to vary from culture to culture, and from city to city, untouched by the homogenizing effects of mass communications. When I set off for the massage district I certainly don't know what to expect, except that I am not anticipating any hanky-panky (for that, the Taiwanese go to barber shops, which are therefore as ubiquitous as bank branches in Canada). I find myself surprised and delighted with a very small but perfect illustration of the workaholic business culture that has made this island such a success story both materially and culturally in such a short time. I had often observed how Taiwanese, like Americans, enjoy doing two things at once as they race through the day, trying to maximize every opportunity. In America's speaker-phone society, one is expected to ingest vast quantities of information from the business section of the newspaper while getting one's shoes shined; otherwise, time is wasted. Similarly, you often see Taiwanese picking their teeth with a toothpick while simultaneously smoking a cigarette. The men's section of the sauna is located two floors below street-level. I am the only customer. I check my clothes in a locker, give myself a hand-held shower, and then ease into one of the steaming-hot Roman marble tubs. One sits submerged on a tile ledge, gasping for breath in the hot dry air. The policy here, obviously, is a combination of wet and dry steam, which are separate functions in the West. The spooky subterranean room is filled with vapour. One somehow expects a gondola to slide silently by. Or a dragon.

When I finish I hose myself off again, and a muscular young Chinese in skimpy jogging shorts motions for me to lie down on a marble slab that looks like it came from the old Toronto morgue on Lombard Street. Then for the next half hour he uses a series of loofah-like gloves to scrub away the dead skin-cells. These mittens have the roughness of diamond-drill sandpaper, and he uses the same ones on every inch of me, face, back, torso, legs, genitals. Then I am whisked away by a middle-aged Chinese endomorph whose big round belly, like Buddha's, hangs down beneath his shirt. He takes me to a massage room, where, in the most tender way possible, he beats my poor body senseless. He uses some technique peculiarly unknown to me—not shiatsu, not Swedish—but perhaps a spin-off from one of the martial arts. It requires remarkable strength in the masseur and a great deal of agility as well. He becomes in fact a contortionist. At one point in his routine he is up on the table with both knees implanted in the small of my back, while with his left foot he stretches my right leg as wide as it will go (farther than I thought it ever would) and with his left hand performs the same function on my right arm. At this moment, as I stifle a cry of pain, he begins talking in a loud state of animation, laughing and joking. I am able to crane my neck around just enough to see that it isn't me he's addressing: he's talking into a cellphone which he holds in his free hand. Just another business deal no doubt, routinely consummated in the course of a routine chiropractic torture session.

I am beginning to feel that the charms of Taipei are easily exhausted. Konrad, too, is betraying some eagerness to begin the journey down the rugged east coast. For him, this will be a holiday. For me, of course, it will complete my discontinuous tour around the island and fulfill the purpose of my visits. A railway runs part of the way, largely a convenience for the east coast cement industry, its employees, and the denizens of the various little company-towns. It weaves in and out of the narrow coastal shelf and the Central Mountains, so it isn't ideally suited to what I want to do. Nor is it anything like a ring-road in its completeness. Indeed, one section of railway recently went bankrupt in the wave of privatization that is attacking Taiwan, including the giant state shipyards and steel mills on the opposite coast that I toured during my previous visit. There is also an informal system of ferries round much if not all of Taiwan, but although their ports of call are more numerous on the remote eastern shore than on the western, they don't cling to the shore—the reefs and currents make that proposition too treacherous. So the best means of going down (or up) the Pacific side of Taiwan is by car, along the provincial highway, without doubt the curviest road I've ever travelled. It is breath-taking and hair-raising by turns, paved all the way and for the most part two lanes. At some places it is being widened and at a few other points it funnels down to one lane as a matter of habit, quite apart from the incessant rock-slides and mud-slides most of the year. Only constant vigilance, and lots of heavy equipment stationed at strategic points along the way, keep this extraordinary highway open.

Konrad and I slip into the twenty-four-hour stream of traffic and strike out for Keelung on the northeast coast, sixteen kilometres distant. Keelung is to Taipei as Yokohama is to Tokyo and Long Beach is to Los Angeles: the indispensable port city. The two places have very nearly—but not quite—grown into a single conurbation. On our way out of town, we pass the domestic airport, and I point out the two anti-aircraft guns on the roof of one of the main buildings. Konrad looks embarrassed. "Left over from past times," he says, "and very old-fashioned."

For kilometre after kilometre, we see buildings being torn down (or rather, being allowed to fall down) while new ones are hurriedly built. Construction cranes dot the city; even as the countryside begins to reassert itself feebly, we see huge stockpiles of building materials—hectares of rebar, for example—stuck out in the middle of nowhere.

Inside Taipei itself, the Keelung River is domesticated: not straightened but given a concrete canal in which to flow. Now it reverts to its old clothes. There are sandbars at some of the elbows and patches of rough water that glitter in the morning sunshine. Here there are bridges that carry pipelines as well as bridges that carry vehicular traffic. Mountains loom in the distance. Loom, I think, is the correct verb. The peaks are lined up in ranks, three and four deep, each one a little fainter than the last: a watercolourist's dream. Along the way are tacky hamlets a hundred or so metres long—rough cement buildings, sometimes with sandbags or old tyres to hold the plastic sheets or corrugated metal roofs in place, running along both sides of the highway (but with no cross streets to form a plat). In many of these villages, empty ship-rail containers are set down right by the side of the highway, presumably to rust, though I suspect that people are living in some of them. In one or two places we pass containers stacked three and four high and many more deep, at a distance giving the suggestion of multicoloured condos.

Almost every village has a business that sells what look like elaborately decorated archery targets on tripods but are actually festival offerings meant to commemorate the opening of a new restaurant or some other small enterprise and bring it good fortune. Many places of business are hung with paper lanterns including some in the shape of pineapples, the universal sign of welcome.

"Are these because of the recent holiday?" I ask.

Konrad laughs. "No, I think people hang them out to welcome visitors to their new shop when it opens, but many have been there for years. They have not removed them, maybe because they are lazy or perhaps because they don't want to remove the luck it has brought them." He laughs again. I guess it's like people who still have their outdoor Christmas lights hanging up in July.

As we near the start of the coastal highway the foliage becomes giant-sized—huge ferns and palm leaves—and bamboo is more in evidence. Keelung doesn't magically appear at the end of the road but materializes in a slow cross-fade of nature and anti-nature, announcing itself with a vast tank farm. As a city, Keelung seems to offer little for the eye as we drive through it, turn right, and begin our descent down the coast.

This stretch of the coast reminds me of Cornwall. Yes, that's it exactly, a kind of subtropical Cornwall. The surf bangs against the land, demanding admittance; the wind has cut some rocks off from the main mass and turned them into tall cones as though on a potter's wheel. Small wooden fishing boats, their hulls painted cerulean blue, rise and fall, rise and fall.

This may well be one of the most crooked highways on earth. Turns pile upon turns until you're no longer sure of the compass, or wouldn't be if it weren't for the Pacific (here, the colour of Windex) always over your left shoulder. The engineers who built the road weren't actually practising the engineering of least resistance. I begin to keep track of the tunnels we go through—many of them long and slithery—but lose track after twenty-something.

But the remarkable fact about the coast—one could extend the statement to all of Taiwan, in fact—is that it is so variegated and surprising within the overall context of its small size and relative homogeneity. At Fulung, for example, comes the first in a series of extraordinarily beautiful (and under-utilized) beaches: vast circles of fine pale sand, seemingly painted in great arching strokes of the brush. Another is at Toucheng, only thirty kilometres farther along, where on a reasonably clear day you can see the outlines of Kieisha, or Turtle Island, so named because its northern part does indeed look like a turtle's head. In between these two points, however, the road is all up and down and left and right, and the very geography appears to change several times. At certain places the limestone and the compound rock give way to little outcroppings of volcanic stone; fishermen sit on them, throwing out their nets time and again in a fine spray. The wind, rather than work on rock vertically, softening its edges, instead gives it a crenellated look, like the wall of a castle. At still other places, the rocks are tall and deeply lined with furrows top to bottom. These formations with all their rugosity remind me of a certain type of weathered, sagging face—the kind of which George Orwell and the later W.H. Auden are perfect illustrations.

The road makes travel slow, which adds to the impression that the island is bigger than it really is. It takes us two hours to get from the Taipei suburbs to Toucheng, beyond which you start seeing rice paddies and even hay ricks when the road dips down to sea-level. By now I know that my attempt at heading off a chest infection by taking dry steam and trebling up on vitamins has not worked. In fact I begin to fear that I am about to be the latest victim of the viral pneumonia that is sweeping certain parts of the island. I can't stop coughing, a deep basso profundo cough accompanied each time by a strangely mechanical rattling which hangs on, like a metallic echo, until the next round. I make an executive decision to use the antibiotics I always make a point of carrying on long foreign trips. What I have in my hypochondriac's bag, along with surgical gloves and emergency sutures, is a course of tetracycline, a drug to which many of the better educated pneumonia bacilli are now immune, but a broad-enough-spectrum medication with which, with luck, I might do myself some good over the next week. At the moment, I'm sweating like a sieve and my left hand is shaking uncontrollably.

There is not much traffic on the highway. A substantial portion of the coaches we pass are decorated to indicate that they contain groups of pilgrims, travelling to visit the towns associated with particular deities. But now a different kind of group outing starts to become obvious: the package tour of Japanese mirth-makers. We are nearing the turn-off for Taroko National Park, which contains Taroko Gorge, perhaps Taiwan's best known scenic wonder. I too want to see it and so we agree to detour for a couple of hours.

The road into the park is itself quite an attraction. It was built in the 1950s by the one-million-strong Nationalist Army who were between communist invasions at the time. There is a bust honouring the military engineer in charge, as indeed there should be. At certain spots the road is less than two vehicles in width, with precipitous drops of, I don't know, thousands of metres certainly. At one place there's a long single-lane tunnel, with stop lights at both ends, though part of the road is being improved. Welders are at work on a steel tube that will form the basis of a new tunnel; their torches piss orange sparks in all directions.

The gorge is indeed a remarkable place, a long and incredibly deep and winding canyon whose blue-grey limestone sides are full of swallows' caves and mossy overhangs. Unlike the famous Three Gorges on the Yangtze (which the People's Republic is now destroying, by making way for a hydroelectric project), the Taroko is not navigable. But it's obvious that the water has raged out of control over the millennia, imparting a sort of black swirl to many of the rock faces. Knuckles whiten when you look up or down. I am struck by the presence of a two-tiered pool of jade-green water high up in one of the mountains, which drains off to make a spectacular cataract that falls straight down to the gorge a kilometre below, as though through some invisible chute.

All the cross-island roads, this one in particular, are susceptible to rock-slides and mud-slides, but here, near the gorge, the problem is particularly acute, and that the road is kept open at all is only through permanent diligence by the government. Signs warning of the danger of falling rocks are themselves often damaged by falling rocks. So are vehicles. We pass one abandoned Japanese car that has been flattened by a direct hit on the bonnet by a boulder about the size of a refrigerator. Only two months ago three visitors were killed when slag and muck buried their coach. Higher up on one of the mountains that make up the gorge is a temple built to remember 200 Taiwanese soldiers killed in a slide in 1958. The original temple was itself destroyed in a later slide, then rebuilt, then destroyed yet again—whereupon the government decided to re-erect the temple a little to the left of the site of the original tragedy.

We thread our way back out to the coastal highway, pausing at the park entrance where local aboriginals sell postcards and brightly dyed feathers from the backs of their motorbikes.

I am really starting to feel like hell, and ask if we might stop at a drugstore so that I might see what patent medicines I can find to supplement my own stash and at least mask my symptoms for a while.

Each time a stream struggles down out of the interior and mingles with the Pacific, a little village has taken shape, as though to celebrate the miracle of drainage. The majority are small and aren't even shown on most maps. They consist of the standard Taiwanese domestic architecture, which is unfortunately supplanting the traditional three-*jian* Chinese house with its interior *kang*, or brick platform, and its courtyard. The new vernacular tradition is a concrete structure, boxy, not very strong, and bare of every decorative art but kitsch, with a business, almost any kind of business, on the ground floor and family quarters above. Those people without the capital to set up a machine shop or a convenience store at street-level often make do with hanging out a short rack of clothing, both new and second-hand: anything to bring in a few dollars to supplement the vegetable patch or the corn field or the fruit orchard or the rice paddy. Sure enough one of these villages has a drugstore: not a herbalist's, but a miniature western-style drug counter such as you might expect to find in the lobby of a lesser Ramada Inn. We stop the car and as I step out I barely avoid treading on an enormous and recently deceased rat. It is lying on its back with its tail straight down and its legs neatly pointing in all four directions, its white belly exposed to the sun, as though intent on soaking up a few rays. My coroner's instinct puts the case down to misadventure, probably by suicide, possibly an overdose.

The next sizable city is Hualien, approximately one-third of the way down the island. Historically its claim to fame is that this was the somewhat imaginative site chosen by the Japanese for their invasion in the 1890s, which gave them control of Taiwan until what the Taiwanwese call "the retrocession" of 1945. Two days ago Hualien was struck by a 5.7-magnitude earthquake deep below the surface. Travelling through, I am surprised to see no damage—at least nothing I can establish with certitude as earthquake damage. The loss of a scale model of the Eiffel Tower atop one downtown building would have been a civic improvement.

We are now descending into the broad coastal plain, a place of lonely promontories and migraine surfs, of pineapples and mangoes and the occasional water buffalo. Further inland-turning roads lead the way to Jade Mountain and other climbing spots. But we continue on towards Taitung, two-thirds of the way down. After we cross the Tropic of Cancer, which bisects the island almost exactly in the middle, the air is even more tropical, though the elevation picks up again, so some of the difference I experience may be purely psychological. I am surprised to hear roosters crow—not because it's so late in the afternoon but because, being some sort of animal chauvinist, I associate the sound with more northerly latitudes. For a while, the highway seems to straighten. I'm very feverish now but feel that there are some sights I shouldn't miss experiencing firsthand, such as Sanhsientai, a rocky island, and place of meditation, reached by an eight-hump bridge from the coast. There are also a number of mineral hot-springs up in the mountains, renowned for their restorative powers, and Buddhist shrines in caves.

Two highways actually cross Taiwan east to west. The larger one, way up north, is habitually impassable due to rocks, mud, and cave-ins. The other, in the extreme south, at the place where the island begins to narrow to its pointy conclusion, is a mere arterial road, not a provincial highway. Stories of its hardships are legend, but it's usually passable this time of year, before the big rains. This, then, has been our plan until now: to cover the 200 kilometres from Haulien to Taitung and go to the small town of Tawu, where the cross-island mountain road begins its tortuous course southwesterly towards the Taiwan Strait. There we plan to pick up the much better four-lane highway on the well-developed west side of Taiwan and have an easy passage into Kaohsiung, the second city. All this might take another six or seven hours. I'm increasingly uncertain just what sort of ailment I suffer from; I know only that it's centred in my lungs and I fear it might degenerate into pneumonia. If so, this would mean that I will have suffered pneumonia on three continents—four, if you count Australia, where I once had Waltzing Pneumonia. So another executive decision looms. It's too far to turn back. And too far to proceed as planned.

Ahead at Chihpen, a short distance up in the mountains, is a hot spring with, it is reputed, a brand-new spa-hotel put up by and for the Japanese. Perhaps there might be room at the inn? I've got to get under some warm covers and go to sleep. Yes, there is a vacancy, and it comes with all the Japanese amenities, including one of those chest-deep bathtubs, which, in this case, is connected directly to the health-giving natural spring in the mountainside. I fill the bath. The water, though clean, is the thickness of mineral oil and smells strongly of sulphur, as though the Devil has just entered the room unobserved. Bathed and kimono'd, I crawl into bed and shiver.

During the night I awaken to what I first take to be my own chattering but turns out to be an earthquake—only four-something on the Richter scale. By morning the sheets are drenched and salt-stained with my night-sweat, but I feel that the fever has broken—departed under cover of darkness, as it were. After some strong Colombian coffee (but after politely declining fish and gruel), I convince myself that I am feeling quite a bit better, though my cough, brought back instantly by proximity to an air conditioner, continues to frighten young children and I still haven't got my left hand to be still. Hell, yes, I'm ready for anything now, I tell Konrad, who looks concerned but makes a display of telling me not to worry. He's seen guests much sicker than me, he says. And he tells me the story of a German television producer who had to be chop-pered to hospital after being bitten by something poison-ous—a snake or a rare insect, I couldn't be certain.

But I can't gainsay it: the morning has made me more hopeful. It is a bright day of exceptional visibility, and the coconut palms are motionless. To reach Kaohsiung, on the other side of the island at almost exactly the same latitude, will take us five or six hours if we drive down round the tip of the island, through Kenting National Park. There is hardly any traffic on the road when we start out. The Pacific is at its most peaceful. Every so often we see fishermen (they work in pairs), rocking gently in their small boats. On the other side of the highway are steep cliffs, sometimes with a red-copperish tint. We pass some lazy cattle and also the aroma of cherry blossoms. Small buildings with red flags denote government checkpoints designed to prevent entry by illegal immigrants.

Kenting National Park, which was a Japanese scientific research facility before it was reclaimed by the Republic, expanded and opened to the public, covers 32,000 hectares, and is home to about 3,000 aboriginal people, members of the Paiwan nation. The attraction for Taiwanese and overseas Chinese is not anthropological but botanical and ecological. The park is partly underwater. Its reefs, including artificial ones formed by the hulks of old American and Japanese warships, attract scuba divers from around the world. Three hundred different corals are found here, and a thousand species of tropical fish. For a couple of months each year, when the northern Taiwan coast is too cold, humpbacks and sperm whales migrate past the park, which draws about two million visitors a year of one sort or another.

It's a strangely beautiful place and more varied than I am making it sound. Within the park limits, for instance, there is an experimental cattle ranch. Yet this doesn't seem like ranching country. The air temperature at the park never falls below sixty-eight degrees Fahrenheit and the vegetation, though thick, is not tall. Partridges, which the Taiwanese call bamboo chicken, run wild; orchids bloom and butterflies frolic year round. Abutting the park is the village of Kenting, a nondescript little touristy place on the site where the first ethnic Chinese came ashore in the seventeenth century. Most of the few thousand residents are either Paiwan or Mainland Chinese. One of the town's two landmarks is a lighthouse built by the British in 1882. The other, which you won't find on tourist maps, is a huge offshore rock that forms a perfect silhouette of Richard Nixon, the person who, the Taiwanese believe, stabbed them in the back when he recognized the People's Republic, thus condemning Taiwan to the crisis of self-esteem and diplomatic limbo from which it is only now, ever so slowly, beginning to emerge. "We always seem to do much better with the Americans when the Republicans are in power," an official in Taipei once told me. All the more strange, therefore, to be looking into the gorgeous Bashi Channel at Richard Nixon Rock, as the rising tide creeps up towards the old scoundrel's unmistakable ski-jump nose. "I am a not a rock," the rock seems to be saying, shaking its jowls ever so slightly. Or am I beginning to hallucinate?

I have to cover another 112 kilometres from Kenting and up the west coast as far as Kaoshiung, thus completing my stop-and-go circle around the island. Once you turn north, the road is well-paved and flat and straight in parts. Approached from this direction, good old Kaoshiung doesn't look very attractive. But as we fight our way into the centre of the city at dusk I recover the feeling I had on my previous visit: this is a place that knows how to impress you with its closeness to life and to the outside world—when it wants to. Soon it is dark and the skyline looks like a shorted-out control panel, blinking on and off unpredictably.

Epilogue

While still on the subject of Richard Nixon, my timing was, once again, unimpeachable. I returned from Taiwan just before the big storms broke. This time, they were political storms. If they didn't exactly dominate world news, they certainly made an ongoing international story, one that carried the following message: the Taiwan problem (for such is how it came to be thought of once again) will not go away quietly.

I began this little book with an expectant itinerary. So now I end it with a brief chronology, to remind the reader of what happened next.

On June 1, 1995, the Taiwanese vice-premier, Hsu Li-teh, was in British Columbia to accept a doctorate *honoris causa* from the University of Victoria. This was a week before President Lee was scheduled to pick up his own honorary degree at Cornell in New York State. In the early 1970s, Canada led the way towards change, with Trudeau recognizing the People's Republic long before Nixon did. But now Canada, in granting Hsu a visa, was playing catch-up with the Americans. The pendulum had swung the other way and the People's Republic was being dissed—or rather, Taiwan was finally being given a little overdue respect for its achievements. Such acknowledgements of Taiwan irked the Beijing government. Indeed, if nations, like individuals, could suffer apoplexy, then the People's Republic would have done so at some point during the next few weeks.

By summer, Taiwan had somehow become a subject in the accelerating run-up to the Americans' 1996 presidential election (shades of 1960). Relations between Beijing and Washington had broken down; the People's Republic demanded that, as a condition of their repair, the U.S. publicly reiterate its policy that Taiwan is a mere Chinese province. At this point, Madame Chiang Kai-shek, aged ninety-eight (or "thereabouts," according to the *New York Times*), tottered into the limelight one last time to speak to politicians on Capitol Hill, where Newt Gingrich, the House leader, called for U.S. recognition of a Taiwanese republic. Beijing responded by saying that his remark was a threat to world peace.

All this while, the world wondered what would happen to Harry Wu, the Mainland Chinese who had become a U.S. citizen and had been arrested on one of his surreptitious reentries to expose conditions in Chinese prisons. Also at this time, the American First Lady, Hillary Rodham Clinton, was debating whether to make an appearance at the World Conference on Women's Rights scheduled to be held in Beijing at the end of the summer. At length, the communists released Wu as a sign of good faith, and Mrs Clinton, countering this improvement in the diplomatic situation, did attend the conference, where she made speeches condemning the Chinese for their human rights record.

The best-selling book in Taiwan that summer was *August 1995*, a dystopian thriller, set in the present, about an invasion from the Mainland. The book sold almost half a million copies, largely because Mainland forces in July had begun "testing" missiles in the East China Sea only 100 kilometres from Taiwan proper, a mere twenty-five kilometres from one of the small outlying islands under Taiwanese control (causing the highly emotional Taipei Stock Exchange to strike its lowest point in nineteen months). At almost the same hour, though, the brawlers and shouters in the Taiwanese national assembly finally passed enabling legislation for the election of a president by popular vote (though not necessarily a new president, as Lee announced that he would seek a second term—"throwing his hat into the powder keg," in the unusually sprightly phrase of the *New York Times*). The passage of the bill was a great measure of how far democratization had come since 1947, say, when Chiang Kai-shek's troops massacred more than 20,000 citizens, or indeed since 1979, when Human Rights Day in Kaoshiung ended, not in one of the playful miniature riots of contemporary Taiwanese affairs, but in a real and bloody one.

I would have enjoyed experiencing these times from back inside Taiwan, but I also found it instructive to observe them from my seat at home, monitoring the world press. Suddenly there was a 1950s feeling in the air once again. In a long leader, the *New York Times* cleared its throat and made its position plain: "China has embarked on an escalating campaign of military manoeuvres meant to intimidate Taiwan and undermine its president, Lee Teng-hui. Washington, as much as it wants to calm troubled relations with Beijing, must firmly signal its opposition to this campaign." In Britain, the *Economist* went so far as to run an imitation communist poster on its cover with the tag-line "Containing China." The inflection was unequivocal. Not "Containing *China*" or even "Containing China?" with a question mark, but rather a flat statement of what the *Economist* believes to be a bald necessity.

Suddenly, I felt as though I was back on Quemoy where, for years, the young soldiers were ordered to wear earplugs at all times to blot out the sound of the communist propaganda broadcast from the Mainland and where I saw rusty tin cans still strung on barbed wire by the tide-line—the first line of defence against an amphibious assault. Past and present, quaintness and danger, were mingled once again, causing a sensation that I now associate with my journeys around Taiwan.